# Protect Yourself from Business Lawsuits

*(. . . and Lawyers Like Me)*

T<small>HOMAS</small> A. S<small>CHWEICH</small>

SCRIBNER

SCRIBNER
1230 Avenue of the Americas
New York, NY 10020

SCRIBNER and design are trademarks of Simon & Schuster Inc.

DESIGNED BY ERICH HOBBING

Text set in Caledonia

Manufactured in the United States of America

1   3   5   7   9   10   8   6   4   2

Library of Congress Cataloging-in-Publication Data
Schweich, Thomas A., 1960–
Protect yourself from business lawsuits . . . and lawyers like me/by Thomas A. Schweich.
p.   cm.
Includes bibliographical references and index.
1. Corporation law—United States—Popular works. 2. Actions and defenses—United States—
Popular works. 3. Business law—United States. I. Title.
KF1416.S39   1998
346.73'066—dc21                    98–6158
CIP

ISBN 0-684-85267-5

To Kathy, Emilie, and T.J.

# ACKNOWLEDGMENTS

The author would like to thank the attorneys and business executives whose ideas, anecdotes, and advice contributed to the writing of this book. Special thanks to my partners at Bryan Cave and to the following people and companies:

David R. Aplington, BJC Health System
Lisa Graivier Barnes, Anheuser-Busch Companies, Inc.
Senator John C. Danforth
Senator Alan J. Dixon
Graham F. Fuller, Rolls-Royce plc
Eric P. Newman, Edison Brothers Stores
James C. Palmer, The Beekman Estate
Alan E. Peterson, Tucker Alan Inc.
John W. Walbran, The Boeing Company

I would also like to express my gratitude to those who made the publication of this book possible: my agent, Aaron Priest, and his brother, Richard Priest; my editor, Blythe Grossberg; the copy editors, Estelle Laurence and Angella Baker; and the publisher of Scribner, Susan Moldow. Working with you has been a wonderful lesson in quality, commitment, and professionalism.

# AUTHOR'S NOTE

Unless otherwise stated, the anecdotes in the book are based on true stories from my own practice, the experiences of colleagues and acquaintances, or public sources. I have in some cases made minor alterations (to dates, locations, product lines, etc.) to protect the privacy of the parties involved. Where more extensive alterations were required, I have so noted in the text. In no case have I revealed "privileged" information.

# CONTENTS

# CONTENTS

# CONTENTS

# CONTENTS

# Protect Yourself from Business Lawsuits

# INTRODUCTION
# The Art of Suitproofing

Everyone knows that there are too many lawsuits in the United States. Small companies often sue one another into bankruptcy. A typical large company has over 450 lawsuits going on at any given time. Thanks to the litigation explosion, legal costs are now running at 5 to 10 percent of earnings for some of the nation's biggest corporations.

People blame this situation on trial lawyers. And for salaries of $300,000 a year, they gladly accept the blame. In fact, trial attorneys usually tell the best lawyer jokes.

The best solution to the litigation explosion will not come from trial lawyers. Nor should it. Most trial lawyers are just doing their jobs. Politicians do not have the answers either. Many politicians are lawyers, and those who are not realized long ago that you cannot pass legislation to make people act more reasonably about filing lawsuits.

This book will turn the problem over to the business community—from the corporate CEO to the hourly employee, from the entrepreneur-turned-company-president to the small-business person. The vast majority of business lawsuits, and the cost and disruption that go along with them, would be avoided if employees at all levels, in businesses of all sizes, simply took control of the situation.

This is a how-to book. In many respects, it is as basic and methodical as a book on how to remodel your house. The book shows executives, managers, and other conscientious corporate employees how to keep their companies out of court. Owners and employees of small businesses will learn how to avoid jeopardizing their companies. Employees of large companies will learn how to increase productivity by reducing or eliminating the cost and disruption that lawsuits inevitably cause. Moreover, whatever the size of your company, by learning the techniques described in the coming chapters, you will greatly advance your personal aspirations as well as those of your company. Understanding how to avoid lawsuits will improve your business judgment and sharpen your negotiating skills.

More important, in today's pragmatic, results-oriented, and downright cutthroat environment, you could seriously hurt your career by *not* following the principles described in the following chapters. Companies are no longer tolerating employees who make the kinds of costly mistakes that result in lawsuits. So by educating yourself to avoid lawsuits, you will advance your personal interests as well as those of your co-workers.

Let's cover for a moment the structure I will use for teaching you how to stay out of court. Most books on legal topics are organized by disciplines as they are taught to law students. They are divided into subtopics such as contracts, real estate, torts, labor, corporate transactions, etc. But this book is not for lawyers, and it is not really about law. Rather, it is a practical guide for business people who want to avoid lawsuits. Consequently, it is organized in a much more user-friendly manner.

In fact, this guide to suitproofing your business is structured more like a book on remodeling your house than a book on law. If you are going to remodel your house, you follow three basic steps. First, you get the *raw materials*—brick, plaster, and the like. Then you make the *structural changes*—knocking down old walls, putting up new ones, and replacing fixtures. Finally, you apply the *surface protection*—grouting, painting, refinishing, and tuck-pointing.

Avoiding lawsuits is an analogous process, so the book is also divided into three basic parts. Part One explains why businesses place so much emphasis on avoiding lawsuits these days. It provides the basic understanding or raw materials that company employees and independent business owners need to fully understand the increasingly dangerous ramifications of lawsuits in today's bottom-line business environment.

In Part Two, we shall make the necessary structural changes to your company by identifying, and enabling you to correct, the Eight Big Mistakes that employees make that cause their companies to have to go to court. We will cover the mistakes made in several potentially dangerous areas, such as performing contracts, dealing with competitors, designing products, handling difficult employees, and addressing the problems that can lead to government audits and investigations.

In Part Three, we will apply the surface protection that makes your company virtually suitproof. We will put up the Four Shields that will protect you and your company from lawsuits. These are preventive steps that you can take to help make your company legally impenetrable. By adopting these powerful defensive tactics, you will make your company an extremely unlikely target for lawsuits. If everyone at your company consistently applies these defenses, you will save money on lawyers, create a more productive work environment, and enjoy your work more—all of which will add to your profits.

Before we start knocking down walls and refinishing floors, however, let's get the raw materials—a basic introduction to recent developments in the legal profession that will put the growing importance of avoiding lawsuits into context.

# PART ONE
# A System Out of Control

"Litigation" is a term that encompasses the lengthy process of filing a lawsuit, developing information about the other side's case, preparing the case for trial, trying the case before a judge or jury and, if necessary, appealing the verdict or judgment to a higher court.

More than ever before, both you and everyone in your company have a strong vested interest in avoiding this arduous process. If you own a small company, protecting yourself from lawsuits may even be the key to survival. During the next several years, corporations will value much more highly than in the past those employees who keep the company out of court. Employees whose actions embroil the company in litigation on the other hand will increasingly be shown the door. This chilling policy will hold true even if an employee caught in litigation is morally, legally, or ethically right. The mere fact of litigation will hurt and could destroy your company and/or your career because of the changing nature of business lawsuits.

There is a worsening stigma associated with corporate litigation. It was not always that way. Twenty years ago, employees and executives often sailed through successful careers despite frequent involvement with legal proceedings, even when the propriety of their own job performance was directly at issue. Recently, I was preparing a crusty senior vice president of a major corporation for a "deposition"—pretrial testimony taken under oath. I asked him whether he had had previous experience testifying in legal proceedings. He smiled, looked down at me through his bifocals, and said, "Son, I've testified before four grand juries; I've testified in three civil trials; and I've had my deposition taken nine times." He was clearly proud of his litigation experience.

There is no doubt that in the "old days," weathering litigation successfully was a badge of experience, almost a rite of passage in many corporate cultures. The reason was simple. Litigation meant the company was tough and principled and that it would get what it was entitled to have. Trial lawyers and individual executives often earned the same reputation. The halls of major law firms are filled with senior trial lawyers who tell tale after tale of corporate executives who booted unruly competitors, subcontractors, or union representatives out of their offices—often calling security to escort them off the premises while yelling a trial lawyer's favorite cliché: "See you in court!"

## THE OLD ASSUMPTIONS ABOUT THE LAW: JUSTICE, LIMITS, FUNDS, AND LAWYERS AS FRIENDS

The outdated perception of corporate litigation as both noble and normal was founded upon four basic assumptions: confidence in a just outcome; well-defined limits on the scope of the litigation process; sufficient funds to pursue or defend a lawsuit; and a close, personal relationship between the company and its trial lawyer. In many, if not most, cases, these assumptions no longer hold true.

### THE DECLINE OF JUSTICE

In the past, a company's willingness to test the propriety of its conduct in court was founded upon the belief that American courts deliver justice. At one time, there was faith in the corporate world that the judicial system was always fair. That faith has eroded, and rightfully so.

A company can no longer have faith that it will be vindicated or rewarded just because its conduct was legal, ethical, or within the bounds of its contracts. Some politicians and scholars like to blame judges for the problems facing the system, but not a single practicing attorney whom I interviewed had serious complaints about the fairness and competence of American judges. Indeed, the erosion of justice in business cases has virtually nothing to do with the quality of judges, or the judicial activism for which politicians and law professors criticize the legal system.

Rather, the problem is the sheer volume of cases in the court system. The American judiciary is overwhelmed. While the American judicial system remains the most just on earth, and American judges remain as a group the most incorruptible on earth, the system is simply too overloaded to ensure justice consistently.

Take federal trial courts, for example. The federal system had over 300,000 new cases filed in 1996, up from about 250,000 in 1990. That means that the typical federal judge was assigned 471 new cases. These cases were added to his or her already crowded docket of pending cases. That same judge completed just 27 trials.

The statistics speak for themselves: the judge simply does not have time for your case. Lawyers have gotten used to appearing in court on the same case before the same judge within a month's time and finding that the judge does not even remember the names of the attorneys, much less the clients or anything at all about the case.

When a successful attorney writes a brief in support of his or her client's position, often the first argument to the judge is not why the client is right but rather why the ruling sought is the most convenient one for the judge! Trial attorneys know that, like all people faced with an overwhelming amount of work, judges will often look for the easiest solution within the bounds of the law. If there is a safe way—one that is legally justifiable and not likely to result in a reversal by an appellate judge—to transfer a case to another judge, dismiss a case on a technicality, or enter summary judgment (that is, decide that a party wins without a trial), the judge will feel a lot of pressure to follow that course of action. If, on the other hand, the request made by an attorney requires the judge to hold a lengthy hearing or write a complex opinion, that attorney will often lose—even if that attorney's argument was well reasoned, well written, and extremely expensive for the client.

Many judges will also pressure parties to settle cases, even when they know little if anything about the case. They push for a compromise that is worse than you want and better than the other side wants, sometimes with little regard for the facts or the law. They just want the case to go away, and often the litigating parties bow to the pressure. Their reasoning is that if you are just going to settle the case in the middle anyway (as happens with the vast majority of business cases), then why go through the entire costly and time-consuming litigation process? Why not settle it before the lawyers take their millions?

Most judges are conscientious and honest. The problem is that they will exhibit these qualities only during the two minutes that they have to address your case. That means that trying to obtain justice these days is always a very big gamble.

## LAWSUITS UNLIMITED

Some lawyers like to compare corporate litigation to boxing. Like boxing, litigation is a tactical process of punch and counterpunch, punctuated with breaks. You can adopt a strategy of wearing the other side down or you can go for a quick knockout. However, the similarities between boxing and litigation end there. In boxing, the rules are simple. The entire WBF rule book is only twenty pages long. And the rules are strictly enforced by the referees and the boxing commission. In boxing, the simplicity of the rules combined with their strict enforcement means that the event is well controlled.

In litigation, however, the rules are much more elaborate and continue to grow (the federal rules were 266 pages at last count), but they are not consistently enforced. The increasing complexity of litigation rules combined with decreasing consistency in their enforcement means that the once-clear limits on the scope of lawsuits have given way to a free-for-all. We have already seen that the referee in litigation, the trial court judge, is trying to cover several hundred matches at once. That means that a lot of low blows go unnoticed. Indeed, there are a whole series of litigious tactics that are against the rules, but, as many lawyers know all too well, are not serious enough in isolation to warrant the attention of the judge. In my own practice, I have seen lawyers get away with lying about whether they had access to witnesses, failing to produce relevant documents to the other side, backdating important documents that were late, and committing many other similar ethical offenses—even though they were caught red-handed. Many lawyers know just how far they can go before a busy judge will come down on them, and they get away with violation after violation of the rules of litigation and professional ethics. These actions offend and disillusion the majority of lawyers and clients who play by the rules and further undermine the perception that justice is served in our system.

Changes to the law itself have also expanded the limits of litigation. Business disputes used to focus on the terms of the contract between two parties. Over the past several decades, however, courts have increasingly accepted nebulous "business tort" causes of action—lawsuits claiming allegedly intentional wrongdoing by companies in connection with the performance or termination of business agreements. Claims for fraud, "unfair competition," and interference with business relationships can now be pursued on very flimsy facts, and, when an unscrupulous lawyer is involved, they often go forward on mere speculation. Because these "tort" claims are so unclearly defined in the case law, few judges will step in to prevent such cases from advancing.

The result is a number of gaping loopholes in our system of justice that allows litigation to spin out of control. As we will discuss in detail later in the book, lawyers representing small companies have learned how to inflict a lot of pain on big companies by transforming traditional contract disputes into "tort" disputes involving allegedly malicious acts, allowing them to seek huge sums in punitive damages. These claims artificially increase the value of what used to be a basic, bound-and-limited contract case. I recently read about an unscrupulous lawyer who amended his $2 million contract claim to add a $15 million tort claim by fabricating allegations that the big company maliciously breached its contract for the sole purpose of putting his small client out of business. The judge did not have time to read the evidence showing the complete lack of malicious intent. "We'll let the jury decide," he said. So, although the evidence was in its favor, the accused company had to contend with these vague and unsupported allegations.

Other changes in the law have worked to the benefit of big companies that sue small companies. For example, the rules regarding "discovery" (pretrial exchanges of information and testimony) are becoming increasingly liberal. There is almost no way to limit the access that another side has to your people and documents. More often than not, the other side will take numerous depositions and demand all kinds of marginally relevant documents, forcing you to undergo a massive, expensive, and inconvenient process of reviewing and copying files.

Lawyers defending big companies can often force small companies into submission by posing these broad and burdensome requests for documents and by asking for depositions from almost everybody who ever worked at the company (including, for example, former employees living in Malaysia). This increases the expense of litigation for the small company to an intolerable level.

One game both sides play with discovery is to scour the documents produced by the other side and find the highest-ranking executive mentioned in them so that they can harass that person—though he or she usually has virtually no knowledge of the case—by taking his or her deposition for several hours. That means that if you do something to get your company into court, it is more likely than ever that your boss will be dragged into the mess, and so will his or her boss, and that person's boss, on up the line. In preparing your senior executives for their depositions, the company's lawyer will have to tell those executives all the nasty things that the other side is saying about you. Not great for your career advancement. The same high-level executive who once might have said to the other side, "See you in court!" is now asking his own people, "Who in our company screwed up?"

Throughout all of this, the question of which company was right and which was wrong goes by the wayside. Legal tactics become much more important than the search for justice.

Perhaps it sounds as if lawyers should bear the blame for the unbounded scope of litigation. Maybe. But you also share the burden. Remember that no case is decided by a lawyer. Most cases are not decided by judges either. They are decided by juries—normally non-lawyers like your hairstylist or car salesman. And juries have also changed over the years. First, they get to hear more than they used to because the law is unclear, the judge is too busy to address motions to keep a lot of the nonsense out, and the lawyers try as hard as they can to get questionable evidence into the courtroom. Second, in this era of sensationalism, when emotion seems increasingly to triumph over reason, juries have become less predictable. They often award huge damages for minor infractions; they may ignore evidence if they like the defendant, and they also seem to be more easily manipulated than they once were by lawyers who arouse their sympathy or strike their fancy. And, most unfortunately, there is increasing racial polarization, which could result in an unfair result for your client depending upon whether your key witnesses are black or white and whether the jury is predominantly of one race or the other.

The result of larger dockets, broadening causes of action, liberal rules of discovery, unscrupulous lawyers, and unpredictable juries is what I call the "arbitrary factor." The arbitrary factor is the chance that you will win or lose a case on issues that have nothing to do with the merits of your position. In my opinion, the arbitrary factor is on average about 20 percent. In other words, the arbitrary factor states that no matter how good your case may be, there is never more than an 80 percent chance that you will win.

Consequently, any lawyer who tells you your case is a sure winner is lying to get your business. On average, a good case means you have about a 60 percent chance of winning and a great case means your odds increase to about 70 percent. Only the best case imaginable represents about an 80 percent likelihood of victory. The arbitrary factor must be put into the equation before you decide whether to go to court and before you draw the line and let the other side sue you. It is the reason so many "sure winners" settle at the last minute, after the lawyers have lined their pockets from your corporate treasury. Again, you should consider the arbitrary factor before you go down the path of litigation rather than at the courthouse steps.

## SPIRALING LEGAL COSTS

Companies bleed money. They hurt when they spend money and get no return on their investment. Most litigation results in a lot of bloodletting for both sides. A complex business case may go to trial as late as three to five years after it is filed. Once one side obtains a judgment, the appeals process will last one to two years. Ultimately, in most cases, one side (the loser) gets no benefit for its substantial investment, and the other side (the winner) gets some return after four to seven years of sinking money into the case without a return.

Amazingly, the cost and disruption of winning a case can near or even exceed the value of the judgment obtained. I recently heard of a large company that had sued another large company and obtained $4 million. Sounds great. Unfortunately, the legal fees were *$8 million.* In most cases, corporate litigation is an open wound for the companies involved, and, based on my observation and experience, in at least one third of all cases filed, both parties lose even if one party technically wins.

The financial wounds caused by lawsuits are much deeper than they once were. With clogged-up court dockets, fewer rules, and more unscrupulous tactics by lawyers, it is going to cost your company a lot more than it once did to prosecute or defend a lawsuit. Further still, money matters now a lot more than it once did. Money always mattered, you say. Not true in litigation. Back when corporations were run less leanly than they are today, most companies did not even have a mechanism to monitor legal costs. Money for lawyers came out of the general funds of the corporation and was not carefully tracked. Into the 1980s, it was common for law firms to send their clients an unitemized bill which simply stated, "For Services Rendered . . ." followed by a dollar figure. Clients paid these bills because they had faith in the system and because the fees looked reasonable.

There are a lot of theories as to why companies started paying attention to legal fees. The steady increase of fees themselves was one obvious reason why corporations took note of legal costs. More broadly, however, it was the tumultuous business cycle of the 1980s that caused companies to fully grasp the amount of money they were wasting on lawsuits. The greed of the mid-1980s led to a lot of reckless business deals, followed by a lot of protracted lawsuits, followed by an economic downturn that hit before the lawsuits were resolved. Executives who had been throwing money around on frantic and ill-advised business ventures and who thought they could get out of them by throwing money at lawyers were replaced with a new generation of downsizers and cost-cutters.

The "slashers" put pressure on their lawyers to itemize their bills. They also required that lawyers provide litigation budgets to the company, against which performance was closely tracked. The new generation of executives considered lawyers to be an exorbitant cost that the company should incur only in the most extraordinary and carefully considered situations.

Today, the financial officers of every major company as well as most smaller ones carefully monitor the costs of litigation, and they do not like what they see. Managers at small companies know that the costs associated with pursuing or defending even a single lawsuit can wipe out profits and that the bad press associated with one nasty legal battle or government investigation can dry up the customer base and literally put the company under.

As for larger companies, a 1997 corporate survey showed that companies with revenues of $1 to $2.5 billion employed on average fifty-three law firms and generally spent $3.5 million per year on outside counsel alone.

A different 1997 survey of companies with sales of $10 to $20 billion annually placed their median legal spending at over $40 million, with almost $21 million of that sum spent on outside counsel. The third quartile of such companies averaged over $63 million in annual legal expenses, of which $32.8 million was spent on outside counsel. The median companies on average employed 250 law firms in a given year. A great majority of the outside costs were related to litigation. In fact, the typical large corporation surveyed had over 450 active cases in the survey year.

Legal costs come right off the bottom line. In the old days, when fees were unmonitored and paid from general revenue, these costs went unnoticed because they were relatively low when compared to the overall revenue of the company. The new breed of corporate management, however, realizes that these expenses hurt the company badly. They compare legal costs to earnings, not to revenue. In the very first paragraph of this book, I noted the figure that legal costs sometimes take a 5 to 10 percent bite out of the quarterly earnings sheets of large companies—a fact no financial officer likes. And while there are no statistics available for small businesses, experience indicates that the cost of one lawsuit can turn otherwise profitable sailing into a tumultuous sea of red ink.

Moreover, legal costs include more than legal fees. The actual cost of litigation is much greater than the mere $250 per hour charged by a decent trial lawyer. The surveys do not take into account the money lost from the delay and disruption caused by depositions of company personnel and the incessant ransacking of corporate files. And don't forget the $1,000 per day charged by "expert witnesses" who are hired to prove technical points or damages, and you are talking some real money.

Further still, in most cases in which over a million dollars is at stake, the company will assign one or more of its employees virtually full-time to the case. For large cases, it is not unusual to have an in-house litigation team of ten or fifteen people, and I once worked on a case where the in-house staff alone was comprised of over fifty employees. The assignment of company personnel to lawsuits diverts valuable resources to activities other than making products or providing services to customers. Moreover, the in-house litigation team is sometimes made up of the people who got the company into the mess, so being a member of such a team may be no honor and can be detrimental to your career, as well as to the company.

## YOUR LAWYER, YOUR FRIEND

Until the early 1980s, top executives very often had a close relationship with the partners in a particular law firm. The senior partner may have incorporated the company; that same lawyer may have had a seat on the company's board of directors, and probably played golf with the CEO on a regular basis. The company and the law firm grew together. Often there were even family ties between corporate founders and their law firms. The social relationships between the company and its lawyers meant that company employees often worked with the boss's friend.

While many companies today maintain close *professional* ties with law firms, and individual lawyers may have strong social connections with company executives, the statistics on corporate legal expenditures cited earlier show that the practice of using only one law firm has fallen out of favor with most of corporate America. Just as companies instituted itemized billing and project budgeting to reduce costs, they also determined that they could lower expenses by the oldest cost-cutting strategy in existence—competition. Most large companies not only use many law firms but they are not shy about letting firms know that their fees (and their performance) will be closely compared to those of other firms. Some companies even have what law firms jadedly call "beauty contests" in which several firms are invited to make a bid for a particular case.

Law firms have responded by aggressively seeking new business and trying, albeit tacitly, to convince potential corporate clients to let go of their current lawyers. And, of course, there is now legal advertising on every medium from TV to billboards.

This type of competition among lawyers was unheard of twenty years ago. In fact, at that time, the legal profession severely limited a lawyer's ability to market and advertise his or her services. That made it more difficult for companies to learn about their options. Now competition is the rule in the legal profession, and clients have embraced it.

## A SYSTEM OUT OF CONTROL

The changes in the way legal services are procured are significant to employees who become involved with litigation. Outside lawyers are now truly outsiders. They are less likely than ever to be perceived as part of the corporate team. At best, executives view lawyers as just another subcontractor; at worst, they consider them to be a major disruption. This alteration in attitude has removed what little glamour there once was for corporate employees affiliated with litigation. When lawyers walk in the room, they are perceived as a necessary evil; when you walk in with lawyers, you may be perceived as an *un*necessary evil.

## THE LESSON OF LEGAL HISTORY

As I have discussed, recent changes in the law make it imperative for corporate personnel to avoid litigation because they can no longer be assured of a just outcome. In addition, today's tactics are disruptive and disillusioning, the costs of litigation are skyrocketing, and mere association with litigation can have a negative impact on your career.

There is another reason why staying clear of lawsuits is more important than it once was: cost-reduction efforts such as itemized billing, competitive bidding, and up-front budgeting are not working as well as companies had hoped. Litigation costs, which burgeoned in the late 1980s, have remained high even in the days of budgeting and "beauty contests." They continue to drain corporate treasuries because the savings achieved by the methods mentioned above do not effectively offset cost increases caused by the backed-up court system and the dilatory tactics condoned by the law and practiced by some lawyers.

Costs continue to climb because lawyers are very good at getting a new client by proposing a low budget based on optimistic assumptions. As the case proceeds, however, the assumptions underlying the original budget often change (which is often unavoidable, given the inherently unpredictable nature of litigation). Ultimately, the firm ends up billing the client for a sum greatly in excess of the budget that got it the case. If, as a result, the firm loses the client, it is less likely to be as big a deal for the law firm as it once might have been—long-term relationships may be a thing of the past, and the firm will simply prepare for the "beauty contest" with the next company.

Companies are now beginning to realize that the only effective way to lower the cost of litigation and end the disruption it causes is to avoid it entirely. The concept is just starting to reverberate through corporate law departments, executive suites, and offices of small business owners. The goal for the next century is to structure transactions so that they do not result in disputes, and to resolve disputes so they do not result in litigation. In the next chapter, I will show you how to take big steps in that direction.

# PART TWO
# The Eight Big Mistakes

For ethical reasons, I must start with a self-evident bit of advice for avoiding litigation: do not commit legal infractions, and pay up if you do. The reason I make this obvious point is that the techniques for preventing lawsuits discussed in the following pages will help you stay out of court even if you really are liable.

It is not, however, the objective of this book to help guilty parties. In fact, some litigation could be prevented if a guilty or liable party would just admit it, pay some restitution, and move on. Occasionally, I hear or read about a company that knows full well that it has broken a contract or discriminated against an employee. But the company decides to rely on the arbitrary factor or its superior resources, and it lets a matter go to litigation, knowing all the while that it is liable. In such a case, the company will usually test the resolve of its opponent by going through the early discovery stages of a lawsuit, but as the case approaches trial, the liable party will become concerned about a big jury award or judgment. The case will then be settled.

In other cases, a company or individual knows it does not have a case but files one in hopes of being a nuisance and extorting a settlement. In fact, there are a lot more worthless lawsuits out there than there are clear winners. Most defendants do not succumb to being manipulated by a fabricated suit, and they may even take retaliatory action against the party that fabricated the claim. The case is usually then dropped.

> The only people who benefit from filing frivolous lawsuits or resisting meritorious ones are lawyers. So why bother? People and companies faced with a problem need to look long and hard at the quality of the case they have and determine if there is an absolute truth as to liability. They should then honor the truth. Let's get the obvious cases out of court first.

However, it may surprise you that cases with an obvious or absolute truth are actually quite rare. In 95 percent of business cases, both parties honestly believe that they are right. From the depths of their hearts, one side calls the other side a bunch of sleazebags, losers, and cheats while the other side is saying exactly the same things about the opposition.

The fact is that absolute truth is quite rare. Our perception of events is colored by our unique frame of reference: our family background, our education, our employment history, the corporate culture of our employer, and the extent of our involvement in the particular transaction at issue. This means that you can legitimately perceive a set of facts one way while I legitimately see them another way.

These gray areas of perception have a simple name: disputes. This part of the book is designed to help you avoid the major mistakes that either cause or perpetuate disputes. Some of the mistakes addressed cause disagreements. We will learn how to avoid mistakes that incite disputes. Other mistakes make your case worse after a dispute arises. I will show you how to ensure that your witnesses and documents support your position. That can be powerful negotiating ammunition that lessens the prospect of litigation and that might increase the chances of a quick, favorable settlement. Still other mistakes cause litigation to broaden in scope or lower the likelihood of a negotiated settlement once a lawsuit has already been filed. By avoiding the Eight Big Mistakes that follow, you will keep your company out of court most of the time, and, in those few instances when you do go to court, you will usually get your company out of court quickly with the best results.

Based on my personal experience handling dozens of major and countless minor business disputes, in addition to interviews and a lot of reading, here are the Eight Big Mistakes that get and keep companies in court:

1. Bad Writing: Not knowing when to write and how to write are hauntingly recurrent mistakes that result in corporate lawsuits.
2. Bad Estimating: Not properly assessing the time and resources that you, or another party, need to complete a job is like paving the way to the courthouse.
3. Speculation: Talking or writing about something that you are not qualified to discuss is often a million-dollar mistake.
4. Bad Research: Hiring or doing business with the wrong person or company can get you into court no matter how well understood or well written your agreement is.
5. Ignoring Problems: Problems do not just go away, and ignoring them frequently converts minor business mistakes into actual criminal conduct.
6. Getting Personal: One emotional memo or outburst can mean a big jury verdict against your company.
7. Side Deals: Informal agreements that go against your contract are like litigation viruses.
8. Misusing Your Power: At the time you are most invincible competitively, you are most vulnerable legally.

This list gives you an overview of the major causes of corporate litigation. Interestingly, the same mistakes seem to occur in companies of all sizes regardless of what product or service they offer. Keep this list in mind as you go about company business and you'll go a long way toward avoiding the Eight Big Mistakes and minimizing their impact if they do occur. Now let's analyze each of these mistakes.

# MISTAKE NUMBER 1:
# BAD WRITING

## TO WRITE OR NOT TO WRITE

A Fortune 500 company once spent a lot of money printing up notepads that had the following corporate motto on the top: AVOID ORAL ORDERS. Someone had decided that it was good business practice to put everything in writing. That person was, apparently, not the CEO. When a law firm interviewed the CEO for a case, the CEO boasted, "I never write anything down. That's how I stay out of trouble." He did not know, however, that his employees were being told to write everything down.

Unfortunately, neither the motto nor the CEO got it right. If you write everything down, then, of course, you record every mistake, miscalculation, problem, or idle thought you ever had. Many people do. And you cannot believe how badly an unartfully drafted critique of your company will come off to a jury. They will not know that you were kidding when you wrote, as a corporate employee once did: "We all run around like chickens with our heads cut off; hello, will someone bring order out of this chaos of incompetence?" The other side's lawyer must have parroted those phrases a hundred times during the lawsuit, "in their own words, they were chickens with their heads cut off—that means brainless and disorganized" and "they never got that order out of chaos of incompetence, did they?" Never mind that the company had done a good job on the contract in question; a few careless words haunted that company for three years.

But the CEO (or any other employee) who does not write anything down often faces worse consequences. He or she looks either incompetent or downright dishonest. If a top executive has no record of a meeting related to an important transaction, a good lawyer can make that executive look careless or maybe even devious. More important, I have seen cases where the noteless CEO's memory was directly contradicted by notes taken by the other side's CEO. Juries will believe contemporaneous notes over someone's memory. Not taking any notes has made many important business people with bad memories look like downright liars.

People want hard-and-fast rules and easy answers. So they come up with oversimplified slogans to write everything down or never write anything down. Unfortunately, easy answers usually result in big problems. At the outset, however, I suggest that you adopt a couple of basic assumptions. Whenever you contemplate writing something down, assume that it will be read by twelve jurors who do not know you and who do not know your company. Assume moreover that one typical juror is a lot like your favorite uncle or grandmother. And assume further still that those twelve people will hear a creative interpretation of what you wrote from the opposing lawyer who is paid a lot of money to put the worst possible spin on it. If what you plan to write will not find favor with the unknown twelve people, the juror like Grandma, and the nasty lawyer, keep the thought in your head and don't put it on paper.

## FALSE SECURITY

### INTERNAL VS. EXTERNAL DOCUMENTS

Employees tend to be less careful about what they write in internal documents such as memos, notes, and minutes than they are with external documents such as letters and advertisements. The main reason employees have a lower standard of care for internal documents is that they do not think anyone outside the company is ever going to see them. The common question I hear is the following: how can a document result in a lawsuit if, as in the case of an internal company document, the other side does not have it?

Internal documents cause litigation for three reasons. First, the other side may in fact have them. In some of the most common business cases, such as whistle-blower suits, wrongful discharge suits, and suits involving "noncompete" agreements, the other side is usually a former employee who may have been storing up all of your internal memos for months before he or she left your company. Then the employee hands those documents over to his or her lawyer and a lawsuit is born. As a matter of fact, if criminal conduct is alleged—mail fraud, procurement fraud, health care fraud—a simple tip from a current or former employee may get federal investigators involved. Then, if you are "lucky," you will be served with a government subpoena for all your documents, which often leads to the commencement of civil or criminal enforcement activity. If you are unlucky, you'll get raided by law enforcement agents with a search warrant and your internal documents will be carted out in boxes. It sounds draconian, but it happens to companies across the country almost every day. Internal corporate documents have in fact instigated many legal proceedings.

In more typical civil cases such as breach of contract cases, the other side will not get your internal documents until after the lawsuit is filed. In such cases, internal documents will not be the *cause* of the litigation. The documents will, however, have to be produced soon after the litigation starts as part of the discovery process. Any business litigator will tell you that one of the main reasons litigation lasts so long is that usually both sides find poorly written, incriminating documents that the other side has generated. Each side then produces the other side's bad documents during depositions and any settlement discussions, thus greatly protracting the process.

Most important, if you follow the basic process outlined below for making both internal and external documents suitproof, your company will get the reputation, as some already have, of a company that cannot be beaten in litigation. That is the most powerful lawsuit deterrent of all. You, therefore, have a compelling reason to make sure that your internal documents are written with the same high level of care as your external documents.

### COMPANY PRIVATE DOCUMENTS

Some people believe that they will get some sort of protection by marking a document CONFIDENTIAL, SENSITIVE, or COMPANY PRIVATE. Wrong. In fact, documents with such markings usually backfire on you in litigation. Normally, your obligation under the rules of litigation is to produce all relevant documents (other than those relating to advice of counsel) for the other side, and that includes documents marked CON-FIDENTIAL, COMPANY PRIVATE, etc. Courts have even developed procedures for allowing parties to review government-classified documents. Marking something SENSITIVE gives you no legal protection whatsoever.

Indeed, the lawyers for the other side just love to wave your CONFIDENTIAL, SENSITIVE, and COMPANY PRIVATE documents at the jury because the markings make it look like your company has something to hide. I have seen lawyers use these documents as evidence of all kinds of crazy plots, and jurors will believe them. As far as a trial lawyer is concerned, marking a document COMPANY PRIVATE is equivalent to marking it "here's the juicy document that has all of our bad intentions in it." And those big multicolored CONFIDENTIAL cover sheets that sometimes go on top of sensitive documents will really wake up the jury, giving them cause to imagine all kinds of evil intentions on the part of your company. Think twice before putting such self-important, legally useless markings on your documents.

Indeed, the only really useful markings are for documents that contain company proprietary information, such as secret technology or financial data. Such documents should contain applicable patent, trademark, or copyright notices. Otherwise, these documents should be marked simply PROPRIETARY. You will probably still have to produce them for the other side, but a court will provide you with protection against the misuse or public disclosure of the information contained in these documents.

## SPECIFIC TYPES OF DANGEROUS DOCUMENTS

The following types of documents frequently show up in court as exhibits because they tend to be the most poorly written.

## E-MAIL

What people put in e-mail is amazing. Consequently, e-mail (including cc-mail) has become exhibits A, B, and C in many business lawsuits. Every e-mail you write or see that relates in any way to the case is fair game. The other side gets them all.

## MISTAKE NUMBER 1: BAD WRITING

The reason e-mail has become such valuable evidence for the other side is that people exercise even less caution when they write e-mail than when they write other corporate internal documents. E-mail is informal and easy to send to anyone. Also, e-mail seems almost anonymous since you do not actually have to face the person to whom you are sending it. Consequently, people do not think too hard before they write an e-mail; they certainly do not write second drafts. They just type and click, type and click. And, depending upon what kind of computer system your company has, it may be impossible to erase whatever you put into an e-mail. Even after you "delete" an e-mail, it often finds a home out in cyberspace and remains forever retrievable.

It is the informality of e-mail that makes people so careless in what they write. That built-in carelessness is unfortunate; it would seem that people would be most cautious when using a medium that involves quick interchanges of information and almost unlimited accessibility. As a responsible corporate employee, you must raise your level of caution for e-mail to match that of any external correspondence you generate.

That means e-mail should not be used as an outlet to complain to a friend or co-worker. E-mail is a poor means to get across a viewpoint that has been otherwise ignored. Write a constructive memo instead. E-mail should not be a tool for gossip about co-workers or upper management. Most important, e-mail is not an appropriate means of verifying rumors. Complaints, gossip, rumors, and angry viewpoints frequently appear in corporate e-mails, and these seemingly innocuous messages have cost companies millions of dollars in verdicts, judgments, and settlements. Taken out of context, one bad e-mail can ruin a very good case. So think twice before you vent your emotions in an e-mail. While it may take some of the fun out of the medium, you should use e-mail with great care and only to advance company business.

# THE EIGHT BIG MISTAKES

## MEETING MINUTES

Meetings are also a common cause of litigation because almost by definition, they involve the reconciliation of opposing viewpoints. Meeting minutes concretely record differences. Differences may be noted even if a consensus was reached to resolve the issue at hand.

Internal company meetings present different risks than meetings with other companies. When you are dealing with other parties, rest assured that they will write up minutes that are slanted to their interests—sometimes vastly so. I have on several occasions had the opportunity to compare my opponent's "draft" meeting minutes with the final minutes agreed to by the parties. The first thing I have noted is that people often try to alter the minutes to reflect something that they wish they had said in the meeting, but did not. I once caught someone adding to the second draft of some minutes language to the effect that my client had agreed to do a whole lot of extra work at no cost. It later came out that the parties had not even discussed this at the meeting!

Consequently, when meeting with other companies, always ask whether they intend to keep meeting minutes, and, if so, request a copy. When you receive the draft minutes, read them carefully, and promptly put any exceptions that you have in a letter to the other side.

Better yet, volunteer to be the party who writes up the minutes, and furnish the other side with a copy if they ask for one. There is a tremendous tactical advantage to being the party that drafts the minutes, even if it does mean a little extra work. When you are responsible for the minutes, you are more likely to take better notes and to remember the meeting. Moreover, if the meeting becomes an issue, as the official minutes-taker, you are instantly the most credible witness—and the other side knows it. Being the principal drafter of minutes makes it likely that your version of events will be the official one. This will discourage the other side as it evaluates whether to take a dispute to court.

Minutes of internal company meetings, on the other hand, are of a very different nature. They rarely help in litigation. The reason is simple. When the dispute or issue that leads to litigation first arises, there is undoubtedly an internal company meeting or two (or twenty-two) in which the company decides what its position should be. And at one or more of these meetings, someone in your company is bound to express doubts about some aspects of the company's position in the matter.

## MISTAKE NUMBER 1: BAD WRITING

Even if just one person at a ten-person meeting agrees with the other side's position or warns against a company action that is ultimately taken, minutes of that meeting reflecting the disagreement will blow a big hole in your case. If the opposing party is a former employee, that person may already have the minutes and they may become the basis for the lawsuit. If the other side does not have the minutes when the suit is filed, it will get the minutes in discovery, and the contents of the minutes are likely to protract the case.

For example, I recently defended a company whose contract was terminated. A lawsuit followed. My client's performance was, quite frankly, a bit shaky but probably not bad enough to warrant termination. I took the deposition of the contracts director for the other side and asked her point-blank if she thought the contract should have been terminated. She gave a good company response. "That was the company consensus." When I asked again whether *she* thought the contract should have been terminated, her lawyer raised all kinds of objections. The other lawyer was obviously worried about what her answer would be. So I pulled out the minutes of an internal meeting, which we had recently received in discovery, and which read roughly as follows: "Jack, David, and Charles thought that termination was justified due to their substandard performance. Jenny said that, as contracts director, she could unambiguously state that if we terminated the contract we would be in breach of contract. The realm of liability would be endless. A vote was taken and Jack, David, and Charles prevailed over Jenny."

While I have changed this story around a bit to protect the parties, the internal minutes actually did indicate that the contracts director gave "unambiguous" guidance that they were "breaching" the contract by terminating my client, and that "the realm of liability would be endless"! From there on out—despite the performance shortcomings of my client—we were no longer willing to settle. The litigation went on for a long time, and the other side ultimately gave up its cash demands. A poorly worded set of minutes greatly protracted litigation for the other side.

You must be very careful about the way you phrase internal meeting minutes. I am not criticizing dissent at meetings. Good companies encourage the expression of multiple viewpoints. That is the purpose of a meeting. But what is gained by writing every viewpoint down in real time? When a meeting involves determining a course of action that may have an adverse impact on your company or another party, ask yourself whether you really even need to keep minutes or detailed notes. If you decide to keep minutes, remember they are *company* minutes, not a record of every employee's personal viewpoint or (sometimes self-centered) agenda. The minutes should reflect the issues discussed and company consensus, not every angle that is taken in the meeting. If the minutes discussed above had read, quite truthfully, "After ten minutes of debate about the other side's performance between Jack, David, Charles, and Jenny, a vote was taken and the decision was made to terminate the contract," that lawsuit would have been settled a lot earlier. Keep in mind that an experienced trial lawyer can get a lot of mileage out of poorly written "stream-of-consciousness" minutes of your internal meetings.

## NOTES AND DIARIES

The only thing worse than copious minutes-takers who do not understand litigation are copious note-takers who do not understand litigation. Note-takers are minutes-takers with editorial power. For example, the minutes of the meeting described above said, "Jack, David, and Charles thought the termination was justified." However, Jenny's notes might have said, "Jack, David, and Charles thought the contract should be terminated—*What idiots!*"

Notes are the perfect medium for covering your backside and expressing your innermost negative feelings, but they can really hurt the company. Few employees ever consider that their notes will be paraded in front of a jury, but they are often key exhibits. Just remember that note-taking is not a form of therapy. Keep them objective.

But you have to do more. Remember that the other side will take your notes out of context. I once had a client who designed and installed highly sophisticated computer software for a big customer. The software passed all acceptance tests and worked well. A few months later, a number of glitches appeared in the program. Because the program had passed the acceptance tests, we suspected that the customer had tampered with the program. Nevertheless, the customer sued, alleging defective software design.

My client's lead software engineer had kept unbelievably detailed notes of the design effort—300 pages covering only two months. Not surprisingly, on several of those 300 pages, the engineer wrote about problems that his people were having with the program.

Noting problems is a good idea; that way they're not repeated. But you have to know how to note a problem. The engineer on this project tended to write about "screw-ups" and "breakdowns" that required some "engineering voodoo" to fix. In the context of 300 pages, these problems looked minor. But the other side edited the notes by compiling the twenty pages that contained the sort of language described above, and managed to paint a highly distorted picture of my client as incompetent. A lawsuit that was going nowhere got some additional life from some unartfully drafted notes.

When you are going to criticize your company in writing, first ask yourself whether the criticism is in a format that is going to help prevent this sort of problem in the future, whether it could be of use to any potentially adverse party, and whether it could be distorted to look a lot worse than it is. If the answer to the first question is no, then do not write it down. If the answer to all of the questions is yes, then the criticism should be objective in nature and surrounded with appropriate contextual information. Here is an example of the wrong way followed by an example of the right way.

**Wrong way:** "Day 24: Another screw-up with the software interface. Called Harry, who worked some sort of voodoo, and miracle of miracles, got the thing to work in some bizarre way that only he understands."

**Right way:** "Day 24: After six days without a problem, we had a software interface malfunction. I called Harry, who demonstrated his skills once again. It's good to have someone that knowledgeable on the team."

The wrong way involves subjective and pejorative terms and phrases such as "screw-up," "voodoo," "miracle," and "some bizarre way that only he understands." The right way uses more objective and positive terms (i.e., malfunction, knowledgeable) and provides the context that shows malfunctions were rare. The wrong way will advance the other side's case; the right way will stop it dead in its tracks.

## CORPORATE POLICIES

There are big problems with the huge binders that contain corporate policies. Getting people to read the policies is one problem, but not the biggest one. The biggest problem with corporate policies is that they tend to be written as rules instead of *standards*.

In law school, professors teach the difference between a rule and a standard. Rules are absolute, like the Ten Commandments. Either you covet or you do not covet, and there is nothing in between. In contrast, standards are recommended models of conduct that can be adapted to different situations, and they can be met with a variety of conduct. Taking an oath to love, honor, and cherish is agreeing to a standard. There are many ways you can love and honor, and different people cherish differently.

Unfortunately, most companies have policies and procedures that read more like the Ten Commandments than wedding vows. And unless your CEO is Moses, your employees are going to break the corporate commandments all the time. I frequently see smart lawyers wave corporate policies in front of squirming witnesses and ask them why the policies were not followed. The answers range from "I never saw the policy" to "It wasn't really applicable to this situation." Juries are not particularly fond of either answer.

Take this example adapted from recent experience. Two parties had a dispute as to whether one was entitled to charge the other for first-class airfare to do a construction job in China. The same company that flew first class stayed in a four-star hotel and billed the customer for that too. The customer felt that the company was extravagant and refused to pay the difference between coach airfare and first class, as well as the difference between a three-star and a four-star hotel. The total differential was about $75,000.

The contractor responded that it needed to send its employees first class and lodge them in a nice hotel because the flight to China was eighteen hours, and the employees had to meet a grueling three-week, fourteen-hour-day construction schedule, which started the day after they arrived in China. The contractor's lawyer argued that its employees needed to be relaxed and well rested to do a good job. He further noted, quite accurately, that a four-star hotel in China is not nearly as nice as a four-star hotel in the United States.

The contract between the parties said the contractor could submit invoices for "reasonable travel and hotel accommodations," and the contractor's lawyer made a pretty good case that in light of the circumstances, first-class airfare and a four-star hotel were "reasonable."

That is, until the other side's lawyers took out the contractor's internal corporate travel policy. The policy had been written five years earlier, prior to the contractor's first international project, when the contractor had very little business outside the Illinois city in which it was headquartered. The drafters of the policy could not envision a situation involving an eighteen-hour flight for which first-class airfare might be justified. Consequently, the travel policy read, "Company officers shall travel coach or business class; all other employees shall travel coach." When the other side's lawyer got hold of that policy, it did not matter how reasonable first-class airfare was for the project at hand—it was a violation of the contractor's policy, and that badly hurt the contractor's position.

This problem would have been prevented had the company updated its policy once it started getting big overseas projects. But it is unrealistic to expect that a company will consistently update its rules to reflect its rapidly changing business. The real problem was that the travel policy was a rule rather than a standard. It might as well have read, "Thou shalt not travel first class."

The appropriate language would have formulated a standard. Ideally, the company would have had a pure standard, such as: "Company employees shall make reasonable air travel and hotel arrangements in light of the purpose and demands of the trip." On the other hand, broad standards are susceptible to abuse by employees, such as the guy who says, "Well, we had to travel first class because of a seven A.M. tee time with a potential new customer." We all know the type of person who exploits every conceivable loophole in a policy.

The most effective policy states a general rule but contains what I call a "discretionary out," which turns the rule into a well-anchored standard. Here is an example: "As a general matter, corporate officers should travel coach or business class; all other employees should travel coach. The project manager may authorize exceptions where the requirements of the job so warrant." By stating a general rule and then authorizing a specific employee to make exceptions, the company will prevent internal abuses, but will not be held to rigid rules that will invariably prove inappropriate in some circumstances.

Many companies have been done in by their own policies, either because they were not followed or because they were not uniformly applied. A great number of these problems would have been avoided had the company written policies that represented a general standard of conduct with the explicit recognition of authorized exceptions for special circumstances. As you review your company policies, you should pay particular attention to those regarding company ethics, benefits, the evaluation or termination of employees, the reimbursement of expenses, and the procurement of goods or services from outside vendors. These are the policies that most often come into play in lawsuits, so they should be carefully written to provide guidance that is flexible enough to accommodate a variety of unforeseen circumstances.

### LETTERS

While company employees perhaps tend to take too many notes and too many minutes, they often do not write enough letters. Never let a letter received from another company go unanswered. Remember that if a company is deciding whether to sue you and that company has an unanswered letter outlining its position on any matter of relevance, the company lawyer is likely to recommend filing suit. Why? Because a judge or jury will presume you agreed with everything contained in a letter that you did not answer. Many companies could have avoided many suits had someone simply answered a letter.

Just responding to a letter is, of course, not good enough. Business letters should always be objective and analytical. For every statement you make, support it with an explanation or, better yet, an example. Feel free to point out anything illogical in the other side's letter. However, leave nasty letters to lawyers. Juries expect them from lawyers, and lawyers are rarely witnesses. But no judge or jury is going to like a company witness who writes a nasty letter—no matter how accurate it is. And when the other side is evaluating whether to sue you, it will consider which side looks "nicer" and which side looks "smarter" in the correspondence. The nicer you look and the more intelligent you look, the less likely you are to see a summons.

Another problem sometimes surfaces in letters. It is common practice for the author of a letter to look for allies in his or her own company and cite them as supporting his or her position, recollection, or understanding. That is a good idea, with one caveat. Never quote or lend the authority of someone else in your company unless you have run a draft of the letter by that person before sending it. It is not okay to cite someone else's viewpoint just because you heard him or her say it. You must let others in your company know that their viewpoints are going in your letter, and you must provide them with the exact language that is going to be attributed to them. If you do not, they may contradict you later on, possibly due to their faulty memories or possibly due to your faulty memory. Either way, you will look like a liar. Having co-workers deny that they said what you wrote will badly damage your credibility.

## MARKETING INFORMATION

Marketing information falls into a unique category of documents because it is designed for dissemination to the other side *before* the parties sign a contract and before the parties perform any work. In many trials, one side introduces the other side's marketing brochure as evidence. Marketing documents almost always overstate a company's capabilities. Marketing brochures speak in sweeping generalities about how a company is an "expert in the field" and how choosing that company will make the project a "no-risk" venture. The brochures speak of the company's "superior manpower and resources" and "flawless track record," to quote a few.

Recently I learned of a company that was terminated for default under a federal contract and was sued by the government for in excess of $20 million for its product's failure to meet a government weapons specification called WS 6536. The company defended itself on the grounds that the government had allegedly failed to disclose its "superior knowledge" about the difficulty of meeting the weapons specification—an acknowledged defense in government contracts law. In response, the government simply unveiled the company's marketing brochure in which it said it was "fully compliant" with "all government weapons requirements." Had the company qualified the broad language in its marketing information, it might have avoided the arduous litigation with the government that ensued.

How to resolve this problem is a difficult question. You are never going to get your marketers to stop writing glowing statements about the company's wonderful products and people.

In the past, company attorneys and contracts people have tried to minimize the legal effect of precontract marketing statements by putting a clause in the final agreement stating that the written agreement is the "entire agreement" between the parties and it supersedes all prior negotiations and representations (including presumably statements made by marketers). Today, however, such a clause will not usually keep you out of court because of the nebulous "tort" claims now recognized in most states. Lawyers trying to get around the clause will claim that their client was fraudulently induced to enter the contract based on the marketing representations, and that is often enough to get by a busy judge and to a jury. If the allegedly aggrieved company is small enough, it may even take the position that the "entire agreement" clause is unenforceable due to the unequal bargaining power between the parties, and some judges will allow that issue to go to the jury too.

There is no longer any easy way to get out of some of the broad statements that employees of your company may have written prior to getting a particular job. The only solution is better communication between your technical people and your marketing department. Marketing personnel are often well briefed on the marketplace but unknowledgeable about the company's technological, managerial, and labor capabilities. Marketing people frequently have little or no formal interaction with engineering, design, and contracts personnel. There must be a mechanism within the company that keeps marketing personnel fully briefed on the company's ever-changing capabilities and capacity.

Marketers also tend to be unaware of the potentially damaging effects of overly broad statements on the ultimate interests of the company. The company must educate them about how their brochures can speak glowingly of the company without making specific, legally actionable representations. They can say that "we have an employee base that is broad enough in its experience to tackle tough, demanding jobs." General statements about capabilities usually pose no problem. They can say that "in the past we have tackled the toughest jobs and met all schedules." Specific statements relative to *past performance* are, if true, not a legal problem. However, they should not say that "we have an employee base that is solid and experienced enough to meet any technical challenge you may give us

without cost overruns or schedule impacts." That statement—
a specific representation about future performance capabilities—just invites litigation as soon as the company fails to meet
one delivery date, regardless of who is at fault.

In marketing literature, you can say what you will generally do, and
what you have specifically done, but not what you will specifically do.
The latter is for the contract only. Again, some basic education instill-
ing an enhanced level of awareness would avoid a lot of legal fees.

## THE CYBERTRANSACTION

Many companies, particularly small companies, pride themselves on
their ability to carry out transactions rapidly with little or no paper.

At one time, nearly all business transactions involved the exchange of
typewritten offers and counteroffers through the regular mail. Once the
parties agreed on terms, they signed a document reflecting their agreement. More recently, offers and counteroffers have been exchanged via
printouts of faxes, and parties have often dispensed with the requirement for original signatures.

The totally paperless cybertransaction has become increasingly
common in business. Website catalog shopping is a kind of paperless
transaction that many individuals and corporations find quite enjoy-
able and efficient. The chief risk with buying on the Web is swindling
by individual organizations that have a slick Web page but no business
ethics—we'll cover that risk in the section of the book on bad research.

Another emerging risk to smaller companies is their increasing
reliance upon electronic means to negotiate, record, and store unique and
often fairly complex transactions. This process, although usually very efficient, lends itself to misunderstandings of all sorts. In a typical case, the
seller receives, through electronic mail or screen-to-screen fax, a request
for information about its products or services. It responds by accessing
computerized product description files, which provide general information about the item or service of interest to the potential customer, and
possibly some general terms and conditions of the sale. The seller electronically attaches the product description documents to an e-mail or fax

cover sheet on which it may spell out some additional terms unique to the proposed transactions such as shipping costs, and that information is transmitted to the potential customer. The customer then sends back a confirming order. The entire transaction is contained on a computer file. This process can occur in a matter of minutes; nothing is ever printed out, and everyone is happy—at least for a while.

Paperless transactions, while quick and easy, can pose litigation risks. First, such computerized transmittals tend to be written as informally as e-mails. People do not usually do much editing or proofing of the contents of a fax cover sheet, and they tend to mix such statements as "hope y'all are doing well" with the terms of the transaction, making the whole exchange look as if it were not meant to be a binding contract at all. If the deal falls apart, you may be in the unenviable position of arguing that the contract consisted of part of a fax cover sheet and a couple of brochures, none of which were signed by anyone at either company. While a signature is not always essential to the legitimacy of a contract, the lack of a signature, combined with the informality and piecemeal nature of the existing documentation, may make a jury think twice before enforcing your arrangement.

Second, anyone who gets a lot of faxes and e-mails knows that cover sheets are often littered with extraneous information about the sender. Consequently, recipients on occasion entirely miss (or dismiss as unimportant) the special information that you have typed on the cover sheet and, instead, go right to the attachments. A couple of times in my own practice, a client faxed me a document with edits; I made the edits but did not even notice that there were some special instructions on the cluttered fax cover sheet to which the edited document was attached. In a contract setting, the customers may not see or fully consider some of the terms to which they are agreeing because they are lost in what appears to be nothing more than a transmittal page. This situation, while not common, may lead to problems when the customers deny the enforceability of the terms you scrawled on the fax.

Third, by patching together a contract from electronically stored forms and documents, the seller also runs the risk of having the terms differ from what it thought they were. Because speed is the driving force in a cybertransaction, people tend to grab files that were meant for purposes other than forming contracts—marketing presentations, technical demonstrations, etc.—and make them part of the contract package. As we discussed earlier, these files may contain all sorts of general representations about your company that were not written with the precision of normal contract documentation. Consequently, by including these files in your transmittal, you may be binding yourself to the kinds of sweeping representations that you would never want to put into a contract.

Another problem with cybertransactions is that people mess with computer files. If you are constructing a contract from a computer file that is accessible to a lot of people in your company, you'd better be sure that no one has altered the file since the last time you used it.

Finally, cybertransactions often omit essential terms. Recently I was involved in a case in which a small company sold a $25,000 piece of technical equipment to another small company. The transaction was consummated through a series of faxes, not unlike the scenario I presented above. Safeguarding the proprietary rights to the equipment was essential to the business of the seller. The initial faxes made only a general reference to the buyer's obligations to protect the seller's proprietary rights. Then, just prior to delivery, the seller demanded that the buyer sign a very detailed hard copy contract that covered the buyer's specific obligations to protect technical information, and that spelled out the legal consequences of improper disclosures of such information to third parties. The buyer objected, saying that it had never agreed to those terms when it placed the order, and the seller then refused to deliver without the protections it needed. A lot of threats and nasty letters from lawyers on both sides followed. Ultimately, both of these small companies spent more money than they could really afford on lawyers because their supposedly efficient, almost paperless transaction was missing important terms.

My advice in this type of a situation may seem archaic, but it works. If you are going to be a cybercontractor, you should put all contractual language that you intend to send to the other side on a clean, uncluttered screen. This prevents misunderstandings about contract terms since nothing will be buried in the fax form. Also, read carefully the cover sheets sent by the other side and do not include vital information in your cover sheets. In addition, print anything that you intend to send before you do so, proofread it carefully, and make any necessary changes in a newly created computer file. Proofing what you intend to send through cyberspace from hard copy seems to be easier for most people than proofing from their monitors; changes that others have made to your company forms will jump out at you more easily on hard copies. Making changes to the document in a new computer file will preserve the integrity of the original file for those who may want to use it in subsequent transactions. Finally, keep a hard copy of all transmittals from either party in your file cabinets.

Printing and keeping hard copies of the contract documents transmitted by both sides will prevent any problems that might be caused by later tampering with the computer files. Having the hard copies will also give you peace of mind the next time your computer system locks up, crashes, or catches a virus.

## DOCUMENT RETENTION

Once something is written down, how long do you keep it? Just as there are people who believe in writing everything down or writing nothing down, there are people who believe they should keep everything forever and people who pride themselves on pitching everything at the earliest possible convenience. I have represented companies whose master files contained draft letters from 1946 still carefully stored in neatly organized file cabinets. On the other end of the spectrum, I have taken depositions from managers who proudly told me about their file "purging" days which occur six times a year.

Unfortunately, as with the question of whether to write things down or not to write things down, developing a good document-retention policy is no easy matter. The pack rats get into just as much trouble as those who, to quote some colorful testimony, "never keep nuthin' 'cause that way it can't git me into no trouble."

### KEEP IT LEGAL

First things first. There are some documents that you cannot destroy either as a matter of law or contract. In rarer cases, there are documents that you must destroy. And in other cases, there are documents that you must return to someone as soon as you get them. Every company employee needs to make sure that he or she knows enough about these special categories of documents to seek the appropriate advice when a question arises. Every company also needs to have someone who can provide that advice.

For example, most people know that you must keep certain information relevant to federal and state taxes for at least seven years if you want to be able to defend yourself in an enforcement action. Other examples of documents you must keep include documents regarding public contracts, which often must be retained three or more years after the contract is completed. Federal and state laws, such as those related to company labor practices or environmental regulations, require that certain records be generated and kept for a specified period of time. Someone in your company should be charged with knowing all the mandatory retention periods for documents in your company files.

Sometimes parties agree by contract that they will destroy certain records after a specified period of time. The most common instance of mandatory destruction is in connection with the settlement of a major piece of litigation. Document destruction is often a requirement of litigation settlement agreements, and these agreements are perfectly legal as long as they do not run afoul of mandatory retention requirements such as those discussed above.

Then there is the requirement that you *not* have a certain document. For example, a lot of government documents are marked FOR OFFICIAL USE ONLY. If you are not authorized to have such a document and you do, even if you inadvertently receive one, you must return it immediately or face severe penalties, including a year or two in the slammer. Similarly, when you are in competition with another company for a contract, public or private, it may be either legally and/or contractually impermissible for you to have information about the other side's proposal. If you get it, you must notify the other side and return it immediately. The marginal competitive benefit you might get from possessing such documents is always outweighed by the potential costs—criminal or civil liability, huge legal fees, and major damage to your reputation.

## CLEANING YOUR FILES

Assuming that all laws and regulations are being followed, it is a good idea to have management-authorized, periodic "file retention audits" during which all employees review their internal memos, diaries, notes, minutes, etc., and determine whether or not to keep them. The same holds true for documents stored on disks and hard drives. Once a year seems to be a good rule of thumb for such reviews. As long as you have a consistent, regular, company-wide process of document destruction, no one will be able to accuse you of destroying documents to avoid their use against you in a dispute.

Guidelines on what to keep and what to pitch will vary from company to company, depending on the type of work each company does. But some general principles apply across the board. Each document must be examined with the idea that twelve jurors might look at it someday. That may require that you occasionally retain a document that you would normally destroy, or vice versa. That said, keep these general thoughts in mind.

Documents to retain:

(a) Retain letters or other external documents that you send to other companies or receive from them until at least seven years after the completion of the contract, job, or other relationship at issue. You must assume that the other side keeps correspondence, and you will need it to evaluate the quality of your case if a dispute arises. After seven years, the statute of limitations (the period during which a lawsuit may be filed) will have run out on most lawsuits, so there is less risk involved with discarding correspondence.

(b) Similarly, it is a good idea to retain your notes or minutes of negotiations with the other party until after the deal that is ultimately reached has been fully performed. The notes show your true intentions as you expressed them to the other side.

(c) Retain for the same time period all drafts of agreements and related documents that reflect the changes you made to a contract or transaction and why you wanted to make those changes.

(d) Retain old company policies for at least seven years so that you can see what policy was in effect when a particular transaction occurred or a dispute arose. Hopefully, these policies were written as standards, not rules.

(e) Retain marketing information that was widely disseminated to outside parties, so you know what kind of trouble you might be in if a dispute arises.

## MISTAKE NUMBER 1: BAD WRITING

If there is no litigation pending, here are the documents to destroy:

(a) Destroy, if possible, e-mail in hard copy and on the computer system as soon as possible after it is read. E-mail has no place in corporate files. If your e-mail cannot be erased from the computer system, consider getting a new system.

(b) Discard notes or minutes of internal company meetings as soon as the course of action discussed in them has been agreed upon. As we discussed earlier, often all the options you considered are mentioned in notes or minutes; once you have a plan, the options you chose not to follow can only get you into trouble.

(c) Destroy self-evaluative or "lessons-learned" documents as soon as everyone has had a chance to read them and knows what improvements need to be made. While some courts recognize a limited privilege to withhold company "self-evaluative" documents in litigation, this privilege is much weaker than the attorney-client privilege that we shall discuss later, and I would not depend on it. Self-evaluative documents are real killers in litigation, and I recommend pitching them.

(d) Discard appointment books after they have outlived their usefulness. They tend to contain cryptic and highly exploitable phrases, and they are usually of little or no relevance to anyone but an opposing attorney after a year or so.

(e) Destroy any writing that uses profanity or derogatory language. The document will not go over well with a judge or jury, no matter how correct the substantive parts in the document are. I will touch on this in more depth later.

## THE BRIGHT AND NOT-SO-BRIGHT LINES

Once litigation has formally commenced, you should not normally destroy documents, even bad documents. You should not even destroy the types of documents cited above that you normally would destroy. The mere fact that you destroyed something after the litigation had begun will come out in testimony and imply that you had something to hide.

Moreover, once a formal request for documents has been served on your company by the other side, destruction of relevant documents is improper under the rules of all courts and can result in severe sanctions imposed by the court against your company, including, in egregious cases, summary judgment—judgment against your company without a trial.

Destruction of documents that are subject to a subpoena is a criminal act. Many federal investigations that were going nowhere have received a new infusion of life when it turned out that someone shredded subpoenaed files. It is called obstruction of justice, and it has gotten many otherwise innocent people in trouble with the law.

It is a closer call as to whether you should dispose of documents, especially possibly damaging documents, when your company is contemplating litigation or thinks it may be sued soon, but no proceeding is pending. While the law varies from state to state, there is often no legal restriction on simply scheduling an additional "file retention audit" when problems first surface. However, this issue presents both an ethical and a tactical dilemma. My feeling is that it is a bad idea to destroy documents right before a legal proceeding. It bothers me from an ethical standpoint, and from a purely practical standpoint, there remains a significant risk that the destruction will come to light and make your company look devious.

A better idea is for your company attorney to conduct a "legal audit" of your relevant files when a problem surfaces so that the company is fully informed of all the good and bad documents before it makes the decision to sue or call the other side's bluff. You do not destroy anything; rather, you just make sure that you know what is out there.

Few companies, in fact, do a thorough file review when the potential for litigation arises. Most litigation is commenced on the basis of the story told by a couple of key witnesses to the company's counsel, perhaps supported by a small number of favorable documents handpicked by those witnesses. The truth comes out a few months into the lawsuit, when the other side asks for all the files and the company reviews them for the first time. Companies would avoid many lawsuits if they knew all the facts going into the case. I'll touch more on that in Part Three.

# MISTAKE NUMBER 2:
# BAD ESTIMATING

Business is often described as a series of calculated gambles. The company bets that if it puts a certain amount of time, labor, and material into a project, it will get more out of the project than it put in. Part of the process of deciding to take a business gamble is estimating. In every corporate transaction, large or small, your company must estimate three things: how much the transaction will cost you, how long it will take you, and how much you will get out of it. Over the course of several jobs, the company's estimates have to prove reliable or it is off to bankruptcy court.

Somewhere in between a bad estimate and total failure there is usually a lawsuit or two. In fact, a surprisingly large number of business lawsuits in some way involve a bad estimate.

It is common wisdom in the corporate world that every bad estimate has both a victim and a beneficiary. After all, if a supplier underestimates what it takes to do a job and bids too low, the customer must be getting a really good deal. Not true. Bad estimates have only victims. Take this example. You want the interior of your house painted and you get bids of $3,000 and $3,200 respectively. Then a third painter comes in and bids $800, and you accept that bid.

You *both* have a problem. That painter is either (a) going to do a shoddy job, (b) going to do a good job painting the front hall and then stop work when he realizes that he made a mistake when he estimated the job, or (c) going to do the whole job and then hit you with a bunch of claims for extra money based upon "unforeseen" circumstances or the alleged "changes" you made to the deal. It happens almost *every* time!

So ultimately, what do you get out of all this? You may get a jury verdict against the painter due to his shoddy work or failure to complete the job. You may get a dismissal of his suit against you for the alleged extra work. You may get a lot of things. But you're not going to get the lovely off-mauve living room you always wanted.

An unexecutable deal gives you a great lawsuit and no product. It is important for both sides in a transaction to recognize and correct a bad estimate before it becomes a problem. That duty to correct applies as much to the party that appears to be the beneficiary of the bad estimate as it does to the party that makes the bad estimate.

When I write about an "estimator," I refer not only to the professional estimators that big companies have. An estimator is any person who assists a company in determining how much it will pay for or charge for a product or service. Nearly everyone at a company—large or small—helps in estimating at some point.

Estimators must realize that their work forms the foundation of many corporate transactions. When you are called on to assist in the estimating process, your job is quite straightforward. Estimators are supposed to determine what the company's in-house capabilities are, what the known risks of the project or transaction are, and what presently unknown but potential risks could arise. It flows logically that there are three basic ways that bad estimates are made: (a) employees refuse to admit that they cannot do something, (b) the estimators ignore known schedule and technical cost risks, or (c) the estimators fail to account for unknown schedule and technical cost risks.

## THE IMPOSSIBLE DREAM

The majority of bad estimates result not from a miscalculation by the estimator but rather from misinformation given to the estimator. If, for example, you are a project manager for a computer company and you are asked to bid on a software development job, you are going to go to the designers and get information from them as to whether they can meet the requirements of the job, how they will do the job, what outside supplies or suppliers they will need, and how long the job is going to take. Development costs plus procurement costs make up the foundation of most estimates.

The first estimating problem that causes litigation is simply pride.

## MISTAKE NUMBER 2: BAD ESTIMATING

Engineers, designers, developers—any of the persons who have to make or write something new—are notorious for refusing to admit that they cannot do something. Consequently, the project may start off fine, but runs into trouble when the product fails to meet its contract performance requirements or specifications. The buyer notifies the seller that the product has failed to meet a requirement and demands compliance. The seller overestimated its capabilities and is unable to fix the problem. The seller then looks to the buyer for relief from its obligation. In fact, a very common claim filed these days in the areas of construction, computer technology, and aerospace contracts is for "impossibility of performance." Companies file lawsuits against their customers alleging that the rocket, software, or building desired by the customer was impossible to design as specified.

Under the usual scenario, the buyer then pulls out the proposal and asks why the seller said it could meet the requirements when it made the proposal. The seller and the seller's lawyers then claim that the buyer did not give the seller enough information about its needs to know that the product was impossible to make, which is sometimes true but often false. Then there is a lengthy lawsuit.

The reason engineers overstate their capabilities and customers understate their requirements is obvious to any lawyer who has handled such a case. Corporate managers have become more focused on short-term gain than they used to be. That means that customers get projects rolling before their needs are fully defined and sellers submit glowing proposals stating that they can do everything. Technology races ahead at a breakneck pace. The short-term pressure on corporate managers, in turn puts tremendous pressure on engineers and designers to say that they can do something even if they have not quite figured out how to do it, or what "it" even is. I have seen this problem in the context of projects involving defense hardware, radar, hospital software, and others.

Ultimately this win-at-any-cost attitude costs a lot more money than it generates. There is no easy solution to this problem in an age when quarterly earnings reports are more important than strategic plans, but it would ultimately save many companies a lot of money if employees were more careful in assessing their capacity to perform tasks. Similarly, customers procuring products or services from other companies must be more careful in defining their needs and in assessing their suppliers' capability to meet those needs.

Estimators for potential sellers of goods or services must make their calculations only after asking explicit questions of designers about the feasibility of the project. Here is a sample checklist:

1. Is there anything about this project that our company has never done before?
2. If so, are we aware of anyone else who has ever done the same or similar work?
3. If not, is the work the logical extension of other work done by our company, and what are the specific risks that may render the work impossible?
4. If the work is not a logical extension of what we have previously done, is there any basis in studies, tests, or technical literature to support the feasibility of the project?
5. If so, do we have the talent to pull it off?
6. If so, who and what are their qualifications?
7. In light of the above, what is the risk that some or all of the project will prove impossible, and what protective language do we need to put in our proposal and contract?

At the other end, the customer buying new technology must ask his own people some questions:

1. Do we have a requirement that we have never had before?
2. Has anyone else ever designed a product to meet this requirement and was the requirement met or were major waivers obtained?
3. If the requirement is truly new, have we defined it adequately for potential sellers to make informed, intelligent bids?
4. Are we willing to make adjustments to our requirements if they prove to be partly infeasible?

As you can see from the final question in each set, "impossibility risks" (i.e., the chance that the project may prove infeasible) must be more clearly acknowledged so that relief is contractually available if the risks materialize. If, as a seller, asking for that sort of flexibility means you lose the project, so be it. Learn to walk away now and then. You will not be vindicated immediately—there will be no short-term gratification. But you will have a smile on your face a couple of years down the road when you read about your competitor being bogged down in a lawsuit and your would-be customer without a product. In the context of estimating impossibility risks, short-term strategies simply do not work.

## COST AND SCHEDULE RISKS

Failure to determine "impossibility risks" is probably the most common estimating problem in business today. The second most common problem is the failure to acknowledge known cost and schedule risks. Once something is determined to be *possible,* the estimating questions become: How much will it cost and when will it be ready? Note that cost and schedule are in many cases inversely related. In other words, if you throw enough money at something, you can usually do it faster.

The same pressures that cause designers to say they can do everything cause estimators to use the most optimistic cost and schedule assumptions in their estimates. For example, contracts frequently become infeasible because of unrealistic assumptions about the cost of raw materials. Often what goes into the estimate is the lowest market price in recent history for a volatile commodity such as copper, titanium, oil, lumber, or even wheat. Similarly, I have seen companies rely on current labor rates for the entirety of a four-year contract on the unrealistic assumption that the union will not ask for a wage increase next year!

Let's talk generally about how to get a good estimate, and then examine some of the ploys companies use to make a bad estimate look good.

### RISK ASSESSMENTS

The fundamental rule of good estimating is that you must perform a standard five-step risk assessment for every job. A risk assessment is an easy but frequently ignored process. Here's how to do it.

First, you determine, based on current information, what a job is *likely* to cost. Look at your current material costs, labor costs, overhead costs and schedule, and come up with an estimate for the job. This is where a lot of companies stop.

Second, draw upon past experience to identify risks that could increase those costs. What are the chances of a strike, a materials shortage, or some other situations that will require more money?

Third, calculate the likely additional cost (or range of costs) for each risk if it materializes. How much is the price of lumber likely to increase if there is a shortage? How much extra money will it cost to resolve a labor problem?

Fourth, determine the probability that the risk will materialize. Look at industry and company data to determine the likelihood that this problem is going to occur and literally calculate a percentage to represent it. For example, a strike every four years equals a 25 percent risk.

Finally, multiply the risk cost times its likelihood. Then add that number to the base estimate and you will have a fully risk-adjusted estimate.

Let's walk through these steps with a rudimentary example involving services. Say you are a house-painting contractor with one assistant, whom you pay $25 per hour. Assume that you like to make a profit of $50 per room per house. You are asked to strip and paint a room, sight unseen, that is 12 feet by 15 feet. You know based on current rates that it will normally cost you $200 in material and labor assistance to paint a room of that size. Risk analysis step one: you determine the likely cost will be $200.

You want a $50 profit. Do you propose $250 to do the job? Many will. But you do not. Why? Because you have not accounted for any of the risks that may cause the job to be different from the norm. For example, if the house is in an old neighborhood, experience tells you that there is a chance that when you strip down to the wall, you will find old lead paint. Now you have gone to step two: you realize a major risk is lead paint.

If the lead paint risk materializes, you must buy a pair of special gloves to remove the lead ($25), and you know that it will take an extra couple of hours ($50 paid to your assistant) to strip the lead paint. You follow step three to determine that the additional cost risk is $75. If that happens, the cost of painting the room will be $275. If you bid $250 to cover the typical job, you will be $25 in the hole and will have failed to meet your $50 profit goal.

So do you add $75 to cover the lead paint risk to the $200 base cost and the $50 profit for a total bid of $325 just to be safe? No way. If you include in your price the total cost of every possible risk, you will price yourself right out of every job. Rather, you perform step four and multiply the extra cost by the likelihood of the risk materializing. If there is lead paint in one out of five old houses in the area, then you multiply $75 times 20 percent to get $15. And for step five, you add $15 to the basic $200 cost to come up with a risk-adjusted estimate of $215. Throw on your $50 profit to get a proposed price of $265.

Note that the result of this basic estimating technique is a form of self-insurance. Four times out of five, the risk will not materialize and you will make $65 profit rather than the $50 that you wanted. That is the insurance. However, one time out of five the risk will materialize and you will spend $275 for a $10 loss. Over the course of the five jobs, you will average your $50 profit without ever being exorbitantly expensive. That is the basic principle of risk assessment.

Assuming that you, your customers, and your suppliers all adhere to the basic principle of risk assessment in your estimates, you still need to be on the lookout for some of the ploys companies use to make bad estimates look good. Here are three recurring litigation nightmares that result from bad estimating.

## Bad Learning Curves

Estimators quite accurately assume that, whatever the product is, it should be easier to make the second time around than it was the first time. After all, if you have done it once, you should be able to do it faster and cheaper the second time. Unfortunately, some estimators view complex projects as if they were assembling a swing set. When you build a swing set, you have a basic, clearly defined task that will go a lot faster the second and third times you do it. Companies often assume a great learning curve between the first and second time they do something.

We all know that large projects are not as simple as building a swing set. There are changing management and resources priorities; there are unexpected diversions of labor; and there are changing customer requirements. In fact, the learning curve on a major project is more like conquering a new and difficult ski slope than building a swing set. It is not that much easier the second time, and there is always the potential for a big wipeout. People do not learn in a vacuum; they are subject to all kinds of exterior distractions and changing priorities. These must be accounted for in the learning curves that form the basis of cost estimates.

The more serious problem is that companies often adjust their assumptions about learning curves as a contrived way to lower an estimate in order to win a job. They try to win business by altering their assumptions to reflect better learning curves than they are likely to achieve. The arbitrary adjustment of learning curves is not a painless way to reduce costs. Rather it is a dishonest way to try to achieve short-term gain that becomes a long-term disaster.

For example, I was recently involved in a dispute in which a company wanted a job so badly that it put a learning curve in its bid that it knew it could not achieve. The company's labor and materials costs were fairly static. There was no room to lower the estimate there. Overhead rates were government-audited, so the company could not change those estimates; therefore, the company estimators arbitrarily adjusted the learning curve to get the bid low enough so that it could be sure it would win the contract. Adjusting the learning curve was easy to do. They just adopted the learning curve they experienced on a much easier project and did not tell my client, the customer.

Then when the company overran its contract by over $25 million, it tried to blame the overrun on my client and filed a claim to get extra money. The truth became obvious when we got their documents; they had misadjusted the learning curve to win the contract. That step got them the contract and a stream of payments for a couple of years, but ultimately all they got was a big write-off against earnings.

Miscalculating learning curves is understandable; however, deliberately adjusting learning curves to meet a budget is downright dishonest and rarely leads to success in the long run.

## THE MANAGEMENT CHALLENGE

It goes by a number of names, but what it amounts to never really changes. A "management challenge" is a conscious decision by management to reduce the proposed bid for a job to an arbitrary amount below what the estimators can support. Those charged with performing the contract must then find ways to cut costs during performance to meet the "challenge." I have been involved in three major federal cases in which management challenges played a significant role in causing litigation, and I've been involved in several other disputes that were resolved short of litigation (but after a lot of money was spent on legal advice) in which the dispute could be traced to an ill-advised management challenge.

Put simply, management challenges are usually smoke and mirrors. The smoke is often followed by fire, and the mirror often cracks, resulting figuratively in seven years of bad litigation. The reason is simple. Parties take a "management challenge" when they cannot think of alternative, more studied means by which to reduce their estimate. Consequently, during performance, employees must rely upon very challenging if not illegitimate means of cost reduction or lose their jobs when a cost overrun occurs. Take this real-life example. A couple of years ago, I represented a construction subcontractor. The subcontract terms indicated that the subcontractor was to perform specified work with its chosen people and it would be paid its costs plus a 15 percent profit up to $1.2 million. Prior to the beginning of the job, the subcontractor submitted to the prime contractor (which had the contract with the final customer) the itinerary for twelve personnel who would do the work. The prime contractor wrote back and defined a reduced work scope using only half the people listed by the subcontractor. The subcontractor of course wrote back and noted that the subcontract defined the scope of work and allowed the subcontractor to choose its people. The prime insisted on choosing the people. The subcontractor then did not do the work, and the prime terminated the subcontract.

Litigation ensued with each side hurling a lot of claims at the other. What came out in the prime's documents was an all-too-familiar story. When the prime was selling the whole construction project to its customer, it came up with a $30 million estimate. Then the plant manager decided, based on little or no data, that the $30 million estimate was too high to get the job. Based on his "30 years experience," he decided that the job could be done for 20 percent cheaper—or $24 million. His "management challenge" to the program was to find a way to reduce costs by 20 percent. So they proposed the program to their customer on the premise that they would spend $24 million and wanted a 10 percent profit, for a total contract price of $26.4 million.

They were the low bidders by far. Throughout the program, their financial reports showed estimated costs of $24 million and an estimated profit of 10 percent. Reality—the estimators' numbers—showed from the beginning that the program would cost $30 million, meaning that they would lose between $3 and $4 million on the program.

In order to help meet their "management challenge," the prime's managers decided to reduce unilaterally the scope of my client's subcontract such that the prime only had to pay my client $250,000, despite a $1.2 million subcontract price. Thus, they sent a letter reducing the scope of work and limiting the number of people my client could send to do the job. The prime had developed a backup plan to do the work itself with help from inexpensive laborers from another country. When my client insisted on the terms of the original agreement, the prime terminated the subcontract, did the work with cheap labor, and experienced disastrous results. A bitter, costly lawsuit ensued—both sides probably spent about $1 million on lawyers and in-house support—and it was largely the result of pressure put on the prime's employees by a manager's ill-advised challenge.

Just like underestimating costs, management challenges often represent a short-term gain—win the contract—with a greater longer-term loss—overruns and rolling heads at the company. Surely some companies have met management challenges, but it has not happened in my experience. Whether you decide to use this gimmick or not, beware that such challenges pose a major litigation risk.

## BUYING IN

A "buy in" is an honest management challenge. It is a conscious decision by management to take a loss on a project for a limited period of time. Companies buy into a business arrangement to establish a presence and a track record in a new market or with a new customer. And, assuming that such a strategy is in compliance with antitrust and related laws governing predatory pricing, in most circumstances there is nothing inherently wrong with a "buy in."

Buying in is a common tactic in such diverse businesses as airlines, online service providers, telephone companies, government prime and subcontractors, and health clubs. A $29 airfare to Cleveland is a "buy in." A

"30-day free trial" of an ab-thigh-flex contraption that looks like a medieval torture device is a "buy in." An agreement to design a software program for free in exchange for profits on the sales is a "buy in."

Customers love "buy ins." They are getting something at below cost, and that is great, right? Usually, yes. And it is true that a "buy in" poses a lower litigation risk than does a management challenge because the seller in a "buy in" situation admits it is going to take a loss, and theoretically plans for that loss.

However, there are litigation risks associated with "buy ins." One is that the buying-in company will go under. I once bought an airline ticket from St. Louis to Chicago for $19. Unfortunately, it was on Midway Airlines, which, without warning, announced it was shutting down about three days before my flight.

Some companies buy in because they are desperate. They have idle facilities, equipment, or personnel, and a "buy in" will at least mitigate their losses. Consequently, you must research carefully the product quality and the financial stability of a company that is giving you a "buy in." The company may have a product that no one wants; or, worse yet, it may not even be around when it comes time to deliver on the "buy in." Problems of poor quality or failure to deliver are common in litigation involving "buy ins."

There is another problem with "buy ins" that may be a more common cause of litigation. No business buys in due to the goodness of its corporate heart. If it did, it would be called a charity. If a company has a good product, "buy ins" are made with the expectation that there will be future profits. Often a company delivers wonderfully on the "buy in" but fails to get the future profits it expected. These failed expectations, combined with a creative trial lawyer, can lead to years of litigation.

Time for another example. Recently I represented a company that requested proposals from a number of potential suppliers to design and develop landing gear for a new airplane. At the time the request for proposals went out, it looked as if my client's customer would buy several hundred of the planes. My client estimated that it would cost the winning supplier over $15 million to develop the gear. Four companies bid on the project. One company bid $0. Yes, the company offered to develop the gear for free. There was one condition: that company would get any contract to mass produce the gear at cost plus a 20 percent profit per gear for each of the first five years after the design work was done. The company offered design work for free if potentially profitable production contracts went exclusively to that same company.

My client did the right thing. It researched carefully the financial stability of the company that bid $0 to design the gear and found that the bidder could afford the proposed $15 million "buy in." My client also researched the quality of the product and found that the bidder had previously designed very high-quality landing gears. The offer was accepted, and everything seemed great until the ultimate customer canceled the airplane order from my client. My client then canceled the landing-gear contract pursuant to the terms of the contract, which allowed cancellation. My client canceled the contract after the landing-gear company had spent $12 million developing the gear and before the landing-gear company had received one cent from production contracts.

The subcontractor demanded the return of the $12 million. My client held up a copy of the subcontract, which said PRICE: $0. But this was another case in which people's jobs were at stake, so the supplier found a lawyer who came up with the theory that my client had "fraudulently induced" the supplier to bid $0 on the development contract by "suggesting" that the supplier would make big profits in later years. These representations supposedly rendered the $0 price null and void. A crazy theory, but powerful enough to cost my client tens of thousands of dollars in legal fees before the subcontractor finally dropped the case.

If a company has the capability and motivation to "buy in," it is looking to future opportunities. When the future profits do not materialize, that company will be looking to somebody to get its money back. So beware before you "buy in" or allow one of your suppliers to "buy in" to a contract. Someone probably expects to get that money back.

## THE INESTIMABLE VALUE OF LIFE

If your company makes any product that could accidentally cause injury or death to its user, this section may save you more money than the rest of the book combined. The rule is simple: never estimate the value of a life.

Back in the 1970s, Ford Motor Company made a popular car called the Pinto. The problem with the Pinto was that its gas tank could explode when the car was involved in relatively minor accidents. Ford knew about the design defect in the Pinto that caused the problem and calculated how much it would cost to correct it. Then Ford allegedly did the unthinkable. It estimated the cost of lives that would be lost if Ford left the Pinto the way it was. Its conclusion was that if you added up the likely damages juries would award to people killed and maimed in burning Pintos, the total dollar value was less than the cost of fixing the design problem. So Ford decided to leave the Pinto the way it was.

Well, the public and the courts got hold of these calculations and told Ford that its estimates were wrong—by orders of magnitude. The juries concluded that by deliberately ignoring a known risk, Ford had *intentionally* killed people. That entitled the families of the dead and maimed to not only the compensatory damages (lost wages, etc.) that Ford had used as the basis for its estimates but to punitive damages as well—something on which Ford had not counted. As a result, Ford's estimates of what it would have to pay proved to be very low and the juries sent a message: don't estimate the value of a life or you will be the one that gets badly burned. Ford ultimately paid millions of dollars more than it had expected.

With a high-profile case like that on the books, one would think that such a situation would never repeat itself. Unfortunately, it has occurred time and time again. On at least six occasions since the Pinto case, automakers have been hit with eight- to nine-figure jury verdicts for allegedly calculating that lives were not worth the cost of fixing a product defect. Most recently, a jury hit an engine company for $400 million on similar facts. The jury apparently concluded that the engine company had intentionally decided to delay implementing a "fix" to a known design defect on its engines until routine maintenance could be performed in order to save money, even though this delay put lives at risk. The damages were reduced after trial to $59 million and the appellate proceedings continue. Still, the ultimate costs will likely be staggering.

The moral of these stories is pretty clear. If you make something that could harm somebody, do not ever ignore a defect on the grounds that "not enough people" will be hurt to warrant fixing the problem. Aside from being inhumane, that estimate will fall dramatically by the wayside the very first time it is tested in court. Not only must you estimate accurately and honestly but you must also estimate humanely.

# MISTAKE NUMBER 3:
# SPECULATION

Another problem with companies is that they all have their share of people who do not know what the hell they are talking about! Every company has the know-it-alls who drive the whole group crazy. You probably know a couple of them. They tell you the secret plans of the CEO; they give you the latest scoop on the competition; they tell you the amount of everyone else's raises. They are right only about 10 percent of the time, but when they are right, you hear about it for a week.

These people are more than just nuisances; they are dangerous. I would bet that they cost your company a couple of percentage points in earnings every year. Not surprisingly, the "speculators" are usually the first witnesses on the opposing lawyer's list for depositions and file searches. Somebody from the other side will always remember a speculator's damaging remark about your company. If the other side is lucky, your speculator memorialized his or her damaging remark in a letter, memo, or e-mail.

The obvious solution to the problem of the rampant speculator is a performance review that gives him or her sixty days to shape up. But there is a more subtle and complex problem of speculation among corporate personnel. We are *all* speculators to one extent or another. A lot of damaging speculation comes from employees who are valuable contributors to the company 99 percent of the time. Often when we say or write something, we do not even realize that we are speculating. It is important, therefore, for even the best employees and business owners to remember some key points relative to what speculation is and how it can be eliminated from the workplace.

My dictionary defines speculation as "theorizing from conjecture without sufficient evidence," which, when translated into English, means talking or writing about something that you don't know anything about. That is a good definition for everyday life. And, while there is no doubt that rampant speculation can get you into real trouble, it is often not admissible evidence in a trial. If you really have no idea what you are talking about, a judge—even a busy one—will not let a jury hear your idle musings.

In business, however, the definition of speculation has to be a lot tougher on the employee. For the purpose of avoiding lawsuits, speculation is talking or writing about a subject when you are not the *best* person to do so. There are, of course, situations in which more than one person is qualified to comment on a given subject, but if there is even one person who is better qualified than the one who is writing or speaking on a given subject, there is an element of speculation to a statement. When you are considering whether you should speak up or shut up, keep in mind that there are three types of comments—all of which may be either oral or written—that constitute the kind of speculation that is both easy to let slip out and that can get you into court in a hurry: statements of probability, statements of capability, and statements of liability.

## PROBABILITY SPECULATION

Probability speculation is a prediction that an event relevant to your business will or will not occur. The statement is prospective in nature; its accuracy will not be determinable until some future event occurs. Here are two examples (adapted from actuality) that have caused employees and their companies some serious headaches:

1. An employee in the design department of a computer company says: "Manufacturing is having quality problems so they're not going to get the computer put together on schedule."
2. An employee in the accounting department of a talent agency states: "There's no way we'll extend her contract, she's getting too old for the kind of movie parts that she is good at."

These statements seem benign. However, they contain predictions about serious matters—a company's ability to meet a production schedule and the decision whether to keep or drop a client. Statements like these may be inappropriate for anyone to say, but they are most dangerous when, as in these cases, they are made by a person who is not the most qualified to make them. In the first example, a designer is speculating about manufacturing; in the second example, an accountant is speculating about the marketability of a performer.

Interestingly, the problem with probability speculation occurs not when such speculative statements are wrong, but when they are *partially* right. Take the first example, the speculative statement that a computer would be behind schedule because of problems in the manufacturing department. If the statement had been totally false (i.e., manufacturing was not having any problems and the computers were delivered on schedule), then the speculation to the contrary would have been a harmless error.

In fact, however, unbeknownst to the design department, the manufacturing department was not having any problems at all, but was behind schedule because the *customer* had failed to furnish key requirements regarding its manufacturing needs until six months after the contract had required it to do so. So, the design engineer's speculation that manufacturing was having problems was false, but the conjecture about being behind schedule was true.

In this case, a dispute ensued. The customer complained, wrongfully, that it was damaged because the company was behind in its manufacturing. The company blamed the customer for not furnishing critical data stipulating its requirements—a very common set of cross allegations in the business world. In this situation it was just one side's word against the other's—until the customer's witnesses testified in depositions that the company's chief design engineer had admitted that the manufacturing department was having quality problems and would miss the schedule. The company representatives argued until they were blue in the face that the design engineer was not qualified to make that judgment, but the customer's lawyer took great advantage of the design engineer's ill-advised speculation. The result was a bad settlement for the company.

Similar problems befell the talent agency whose accountant speculated that the agency would not renew the contract of the alleged has-been. Better-qualified people at the agency decided that it was worth renewing the actress's contract, and they tried hard to keep the actress working during the contract negotiations, but she boozed it up and showed up late on the set of a big TV show. She also threw a lot of tantrums. Eventually, the agency decided not to renew her contract. A friend of hers at the agency disclosed to her the accountant's speculative comment about her age and beauty. The actress sued the agency claiming that, after remaining loyal to the agency for all of her prime years, the agency had discarded her because its employees were focused on younger talent. She was in fact a halfway decent actress, and you should have seen the tears flowing as she gave her deposition. I am glad I was not representing the agency in that suit. The accountant's speculation that the agency would not renew the contract was right, but the reason was wrong, and a lawsuit ensued, followed by an undisclosed settlement.

As the previous examples indicate, probability speculation is most dangerous when made by people who know enough to get the story half right. We are not talking about the company clown here. We are not talking about really stupid statements. We are talking about statements that smart people let slip out every day because they are not thinking about the possible ramifications of the things that they say or write. People in your company need to develop a second sense that lets them know when to bite their tongues and defer to the real experts.

## CAPABILITY SPECULATION

Capability speculation is a statement made by someone other than the most qualified person to make it about a company's ability to perform a task. It is not a statement about the future; it is a statement about the present. Capability speculation is easier to engage in and yet more dangerous than probability speculation.

Here's why. Say that a supermarket owner tours a farm that sells peaches. The market owner is not as well qualified as his produce manager to judge the quality of produce. In fact, the owner was raised in suburbia and knows little if anything about produce. He looks at an orchard, sees a bunch of big peaches, and says to the farmer: "You grow the best peaches in California." That is capability speculation. The owner is speculating about the farmer's capabilities.

Capability speculation is easy to do because it most often involves giving someone a compliment. I have represented parties in a couple of major disputes in which positive, backslapping statements made by unqualified people have badly hurt their companies. In each case, when I interviewed the employee who engaged in the capability speculation, he said he was just trying to make the other party feel good—by giving them a confidence boost. There is nothing wrong with boosting someone's confidence so long as the object of your compliments really deserves it. But if you are not the most qualified person to make that judgment, it is a hollow compliment at best and a dangerous one at worst.

The reason that capability speculation can be more dangerous than probability speculation is that, on its face, capability speculation is an absolute statement of truth. It does not involve anything that is obviously speculative. Probability speculation involves statements about the future, so your lawyer can at least *argue* with a straight face that you did not know what you were talking about when you predicted the future. On the other hand, when you say "you grow the best peaches," there is nothing on the face of the statement that leaves any room for error. There is no fuzz on that peach.

In fact, suppose that those peaches were beautiful on the outside but prone to being bitter and acidic and giving people with weak stomachs severe gastrointestinal discomfort. Any qualified produce manager would have picked out those problems quite quickly. Under the present facts, however, if the company refused to buy more peaches on the grounds that they were of inferior quality, the farmer could sue and cite the owner's glowing compliment as evidence that quality had nothing to do with the decision. What started out as a compliment would become the key piece of testimony in an ensuing dispute between the farmer and the grocery-store chain over the termination of the farmer as a supplier.

The above situation is common but not the most common one involving capability speculation. Such speculation rears its head most often in disputes between companies and their former employees. Consider this example. A young stockbroker works for a large, respectable brokerage firm. Out of the blue, the son of an elderly client of the broker accuses the broker of "churning" the account. The son claims that the young broker is making a lot of unnecessary stock trades to generate large commissions. This is a serious allegation in the brokerage world, and is, if true, grounds for immediate dismissal of the broker. The company conducts an internal investigation and concludes that the broker was in fact churning the account, a conclusion which the broker and his lawyer vehemently dispute. The brokerage house fires the broker and the broker sues for defamation.

Now what is the first document that the broker is going to tell his lawyer to subpoena? If you guessed the records of the broker's transactions, you are wrong. While they are the most relevant records, they are not the most valuable. Rather, the lawyer will subpoena the two annual performance evaluations that the firm gave the broker. Why? Because there are lines on those evaluations for ETHICS and ACCOUNT MANAGEMENT and because the supervisor gave the junior broker an EXCELLENT—the highest mark—in these areas both years.

The fact of the matter is that the young broker was nice looking as well as professional in his conduct, but no one had ever monitored his activities or even known him long enough to assess whether he was ethical. There was a place on the employee evaluation form for the supervisor to mark QUALITY NOT OBSERVED POSITIVELY OR NEGATIVELY, but checking that box by the lines marked ETHICS or ACCOUNT MANAGEMENT would have seemed, well, "a bit cold," in the words of the supervisor. So the supervisor engaged in some capability speculation that proved quite contrary to the conclusion that the company reached just two months after the evaluation.

In fact, often employee evaluation forms seem directly at odds with what litigation attorneys are ultimately told about the capabilities of employees. Often the anomalies are due to capability speculation, although sometimes supervisors know the truth but just do not have the heart to say something bad (more on that in the section of the book entitled "Ignoring Problems"). The lesson here is do not state the capabilities of your employees, your customers, your suppliers, or your partners unless you are the best-qualified person to make such judgments.

## LIABILITY SPECULATION

There is only one person who is not speculating when he or she makes an assessment of liability: your lawyer. Depending upon the circumstances, contract administrators, financial analysts, insurance adjusters, federal investigators and agents, risk managers, and the like might be qualified to some degree to assist in the development of facts supporting a determination of civil and/or criminal liability. But even they often forget the fine line between questions of fact and conclusions of law. The latter should always be left for attorneys. You can be right factually and wrong legally.

Here is an example. A company builds a ship for a cruise line. The cruise line gives the company a detailed list of design requirements (six decks, four engines, etc.) and a detailed list of performance specifications (maximum cruising speed not less than 28 knots). The company builds the boat, but when it is tested, it only goes 27.2 knots at maximum speed. The cruise line demands that the company fix the problem. The chief performance engineer at the company writes an apologetic letter to the cruise line admitting "we breached the contract by failing to meet the specified speed and we shall be implementing whatever corrective action is necessary to meet our commitments under the contract."

This is a huge mistake in terms of liability speculation. A performance engineer is perfectly qualified to say "tests show that the ship failed to meet the maximum speed specification," but he is totally unqualified to say that his company "breached the contract." He is not an expert in contract liability.

The engineer quite logically thinks that failing to meet the specified speed is failing to meet the contract. However, issues of liability are often neither logical nor intuitive. For example, if he then informs his lawyer of the situation, the lawyer will ask him a series of questions carefully designed to determine if there is a basis on which to separate the issues of performance from those of liability. Assume, for example, that the engineer informs his lawyer that his engineering staff concluded that no one could build a boat of the specified size that travels at the specified speed with only four engines. His lawyer will then inform him of a body of law holding that when the customer has provided both design and performance specifications and they are in conflict, the builder, under the law, does not have to bear the entire cost of fixing the problem. Indeed, in some jurisdictions, the drafter of the specifications has to bear all the costs. There may be no breach at all. In other words, to an engineer, missing a key performance requirement may seem like a breach of contract, when, in fact, a lawyer might have a pretty good argument that it is not.

Hence, a seemingly appropriate letter containing liability speculation could cause lengthy litigation. Had the lawyer been consulted first, the engineer could have written a letter that correctly stated the applicable standard of liability and thereby prevented the other side from having the kind of ammunition that encourages the filing of otherwise weak or meritless lawsuits.

When a problem arises in the performance of a job, no one in the company should speculate about liability until the company attorney has had a look at the facts. Once the attorney has made a good liability assessment—one that includes the likely cost of litigation as a risk factor to the company—the company can then make a well-informed decision whether to risk a lawsuit.

I would speculate that by now you have gotten the message about speculation. It has caused a lot of trouble and cost companies a lot of money over the years. You can avoid a lot of problems by simply asking yourself whether you have consulted the most qualified person before you make any statement of probability, capability, or liability. It is that easy.

# MISTAKE NUMBER 4:
# BAD RESEARCH

You may have the best-run company on earth. You may have the most progressive benefits program known to humankind. Your hiring and promotion system may have won a presidential citation for liberty and justice in the workplace. But if you hire someone who is a bad egg—someone who is hell-bent on getting something out of your company at everyone else's expense—it does not matter one iota what a great company you run. You will find yourself in court battling that person.

Similarly, you may have the best product or service on earth. You may have the motto "God, Customer, Family." You may have the most brilliantly written commitments since the Magna Carta. But if you do business with an unethical, incompetent, or financially desperate company, it does not matter one bit how clear and reasonable your business arrangements are. You will find yourself in court battling that company.

> A good work environment cannot overcome a bad employee. A good contract cannot overcome a devious customer or vendor. Yet companies often hire people with very little knowledge about their background, and companies do business with other organizations without conducting even the most basic research on the reliability of that potential business associate.

Hence, the fourth error in the list of the Eight Big Mistakes that get companies into court is bad research. Businesses all too frequently fail to seek and utilize readily available information about potential employees, customers, and vendors *before* making commitments to them.

## THE ENEMY WITHIN

When companies hire employees, they tend to rely too heavily on subjective criteria and not enough on objective criteria. For example, the company often fails to check out the information (or gaps in the information) on résumés. A recent study revealed that over 30 percent of all résumés have something false on them. In some cases, the misstatement is an exaggeration or stretching of the truth, but it represents an inaccuracy nonetheless. If an employee lies to get a job, he or she will lie to keep it and lie to get back at you and your company if you let that employee go. This represents a risk ranging from embarrassment to long-term litigation.

Lawyers are not exempt from this problem. Several years ago, a major law firm learned that one of its partners who had been with the firm for several years had never graduated from law school and never passed the bar exam. Consider how negligent the law firm was in verifying simple facts to enable this alleged lawyer to have gone so far with his lies. Obviously, no one had ever received a final law school transcript from that person when he applied for the job and no one had even determined whether he passed the bar exam, which can usually be verified by calling the state bar association or by reading a list published in the newspaper.

This type of failure to verify simple statements occurs all the time at respected companies and firms, large and small. Instead of doing the work to verify something objectively, people rely on the subjective interview of the potential employee, asking that person about his or her résumé. If the person speaks intelligently and forcefully about what is on his or her résumé, the interviewer assumes that the résumé is accurate. Yet there are many clever people who have a convincing story and have done their homework on the lies in their résumés. These are dangerous people who can wreak havoc on a good company.

Similarly, human resources departments often rely on references to ensure that they have a quality candidate. This also is not a good way to decide whether to hire someone. There are documented cases of people who colluded with friends, citing those friends as phony job references. The bigger problem, however, is that no one gives a bad reference anymore. I have heard of cases in which employees were fired from companies for all kinds of horrible things but in which the companies agreed to give the fired employees acceptable references just to get rid of them. Professors have been sued for giving bad references and now almost always say nice things about their former pupils. Many states have laws that protect writers of references, but there are too many loopholes in these laws to give the reference writer much comfort. Further still, there are few applicants on earth who cannot find a couple of people who will say good things about them. These applicants do not put on their résumés the names of the people who think that they are incompetent idiots.

Even more stunning is that a lot of companies will not terminate an employee when they learn of résumé fraud. Either the fraud is not reported to the human resources department, or the human resources department does not do anything about it because the employee is working out—for the time being.

It may sound tough, but companies should have no-excuses policies for résumé fraud. First, the human resources department or person should, as a condition of an interview, make the prospective employee state in writing that he or she consents to the company doing a criminal background check and taking any reasonable steps to verify statements on his or her résumé such as calling former employers whether they are on the reference list or not, obtaining certified copies of transcripts directly from the university, etc. Second, the human resources department should have a checklist to verify every item of substance on a résumé and should not make an offer until everything checks out. Third, after accepting the offer, the employee should sign a notarized certification that every representation he or she made on his or her résumé or in the interview process was accurate, and that, if at any time anything is found to have been false, it is grounds for immediate dismissal, no matter how many years the employee has worked for the company and no matter how high up that person may have risen in the corporate structure. These admittedly rigorous steps will ensure that you have the right people working for your company.

One additional note, about private investigators. While I encourage companies to be diligent in verifying their potential employees' pasts, I think the actions taken should be confined to those which a human resources person can do from his or her desk. Juries do not like companies that hire private investigators to follow people or intrude on their private lives unless the situation involves very serious matters such as bribery or stealing. Moreover, more than one investigator has gotten a company in trouble by overstepping his or her bounds. Hidden cameras, recorded conversations, and other devices may be illegal in your state. Even if legal under the circumstances, they may still be unethical. We all remember the jury zapping ABC for its use of hidden cameras to investigate Food Lion grocery chain. By many accounts (although Food Lion disputes the allegations), there was evidence that some Food Lion employees had engaged in unsanitary practices. Food Lion elected not even to dispute the truthfulness of the ABC report in its lawsuit. Rather, Food Lion sued and won because the jury did not like spying. Keep that in mind. Be thorough but not intrusive.

## THE ENEMY WITHOUT

Just as companies often do not thoroughly research their future employees, they often do not adequately research the other companies with which they choose to do business. They do business with organizations that have proven to be unethical or unreliable in their past dealings.

Banks and other financial institutions have always placed a strong emphasis on past performance by measuring the credit history of potential borrowers. They know that they are more likely to get paid if their borrowers have paid others back on time in the past. This principle should hold true for companies that buy or sell a product or service as well. Like banks, these companies want honesty, reliability, and solvency on the part of those organizations with which they deal. Yet, in deciding which projects to bid on or which suppliers to select, companies in the businesses of manufacturing, construction, and services often place inadequate emphasis upon the financial and/or performance history of their potential customers and their potential suppliers.

Indeed, the biggest procurer of goods and services in the world, the United States Government, only recently began to emphasize past performance in selecting suppliers. A series of federal directives and regulations passed in 1996 and 1997 require a thorough analysis by

## MISTAKE NUMBER 4: BAD RESEARCH

federal officials of a potential provider's past performance. These new requirements will, I predict, filter down to the federal subcontracting community and then to businesses at large. Within the next few years, evaluations of the past performance of potential customers and suppliers will become more thorough and more relevant to key business decisions. And the better that your company is at this process, the more money it will make and the less likely it is to end up in court.

### PUBLIC VS. PRIVATE INFORMATION

There is a lot of information about companies in the public domain. The first piece of information that you need about a potential customer or supplier is financial. There is a vast amount of corporate financial information now available on-line. Company Web sites are a start, but they are marketing tools that put the best spin on a company. The Lexis/Nexis service, used mostly by lawyers, can access most public filings made by large companies with the Securities and Exchange Commission, including 10K's, 10q's, and annual reports. State securities commissions and secretary of state offices have similar information about other companies. I have learned very significant facts about the financial status of companies or divisions within companies by looking at this information. I have learned which divisions are profitable, which divisions are losing money, which divisions are up for sale, which product lines are being phased out, and a host of other facts relevant to the question of whether one would want to do business with that company on a particular job.

The same on-line services, supplemented by some research by your lawyer, can reveal whether your potential business partner has been sued or filed suit recently, what the issues were, and how the matter was resolved. The pleadings in those suits are a matter of public record and can provide stunningly frank information about the business practices of companies that you are considering for big jobs. Recently I filed suit on behalf of a race car driver who did not get his sponsorship money from an engine overhauler. The engine overhauler had conveniently failed to inform the driver that it was coming out of bankruptcy. A simple legal search of public financial and bankruptcy records would have revealed this fact before the deal was consummated. If the driver had spent $200 up front for an hour's worth of a lawyer's time, he would have realized the problem in time to find another sponsor and would have saved himself thousands of dollars in litigation fees.

The federal government also keeps a list available through the General Services Administration of companies and individuals that have been suspended or debarred from doing business with the government due to illegal, unethical, or otherwise improper conduct. If a company you are considering working with comes up on that list, you may wish to file a Freedom of Information Act (FOIA) request with the agency to get more information on the problems that company has experienced with Uncle Sam. It may have a lot of relevance to your potential transaction. State and local consumer organizations maintain similar information about disreputable businesses and can provide valuable assistance.

When you are considering dealing with a relatively small company, say one comprising fifty employees or less, you may not get all of the relevant information about the company by just searching for information using the company name. A lot of shady operations change names or disband and reincorporate on a regular basis. This practice is particularly true with small construction and landscaping services, small investment or brokerage companies, and small insurance and finance companies. Make sure you learn the names of the principal officers of that company and conduct the same sort of information searches on those people as individuals before doing business with their companies.

The question as to whether a company should call other customers or suppliers of the organization with which it is considering a business arrangement is controversial. Obviously, conversations with companies that have already been in your position can be quite valuable. The problem is that any time you have two companies talking "off-line" about a third company, there is a risk. If the communicating companies are big and the information imparted is unfavorable, there is a risk that the third company will allege an antitrust conspiracy; if the communicating companies are small, there is still the risk of an unfair competition claim.

However meritless these claims often are, companies make them all the time. Recently, I was involved in a case in which a subcontractor spoke to a third party about the desirability of working with the prime contractor on a future project. The subcontractor learned from the third party that the customer did not like the prime and would not likely award it future work. This sounded like valuable information. The subcontractor naturally indicated to the prime that it would not work with the prime on future projects. The prime lost its future work. When it learned that the subcontractor had spoken to a third party about its capabilities, it filed a $12 million lawsuit alleging a conspiracy between the subcontractor and the third party to destroy the prime. The suit was ridiculous and untrue, but it cost the subcontractor $400,000 in legal fees before the case was ultimately resolved.

A better practice would be to obtain permission to communicate with other companies that have done business with the company with which you are considering a relationship. If you are the customer, for example, require that all potential bidders list their previous five or their biggest five contracts for the same product or service and give the name and number of a contact person at these other companies and permission to contact these companies. Note that this is not asking for references. By requiring that they list the most recent and/or biggest contracts, you do not allow companies the discretion to leave out bad experiences.

If you are bidding on a project, ask the customer in writing if it would be okay to consult with other companies that have done work for them. Then you can turn what might have been dangerous "off-line" conversations into productive "on-line" conversations and avoid any allegations of conspiracy.

## THE PAROCHIAL SCHOOL

I have been continually stunned at how often a company will ignore *its own* previous bad experience with an organization when deciding whether to do further business with it. I was not long ago involved in a case in which the other side stiffed my client for over $500,000. When I was retained to handle the matter, the first thing I learned was that my client had, only a year earlier, been involved with the same company on a very similar project, and had been cheated out of $200,000. In addition, the same two employees of the other company who had behaved unethically on the second contract had administered the first one.

I asked my client's employees why they ever entered into the second contract. I was given the following reasons: my client needed business at the time, and the second contract had some severe penalty provisions added for nonpayment to cover the kinds of situations that had happened the first time around. These are quite common reasons for perpetuating a bad relationship. Remember two things. First, it is better to have no contract at all than to have one with a loser or an opportunist. Second, no contract in the world, however well worded, will deter a slimeball. If someone is out to make it at your expense, he does not give a damn about what the contract says. That company's lawyer will invent some loophole in the agreement, the nasty letters will begin, and a lawsuit will follow. You may prevail, but it will cost you a fortune. That is why you must carefully research your potential business counterparts up front and cease doing business with them if they prove to be unreliable or unethical.

It gets worse. I have seen situations in which a division of one company is in fierce litigation with another corporation. While that battle reaches a nasty crescendo, a second division of the first company enters into a deal with the same disreputable corporation. The second division says to its sister division that the dispute is not its problem and ignores the bad experience from within its own company. This is parochialism at its worst and is almost always counterproductive.

Unless the dispute revolves around issues that are unquestionably unique to the specific transaction at issue and unless there is no possible alternative company with which you can do business, there is no excuse for one part of your company to do business with an organization that is dragging another part of your company into the gutter. There is a good chance that the unethical company will cause the same problems for the second division of your company that it caused for the first division. The employees of your second division might insist that they are making a good deal, but those people should remember that the first deal probably looked pretty good too at the outset. Moreover, by giving the offending company more work, your company is saying that it does not put the conviction of the whole company behind the position it is taking in the ongoing dispute. I will have more to say on that issue later.

# MISTAKE NUMBER 5: IGNORING PROBLEMS

As you know, things have a tendency to get worse unless you take decisive action. It is more than a rule of business. It is more than a rule of life. It is a rule of the universe.

You may remember hearing about the Big Bang in your high school physics class. The universe came into existence from a tiny, densely ordered mass by exploding into a wild expanding mess. As it expands, the universe is entropic—it becomes increasingly disordered. That's why vases and glasses fall off tables and shatter but never pick themselves up and put themselves back together again. People have the unique ability to reverse entropy—to go against the grain of the universe—and actually act constructively.

> Entropy means that every second you do nothing, the world becomes a little less ordered. In your business, every time you decide to put off the resolution of a problem, there will be a universal tendency for it to get worse. So doing nothing is really doing something. It is allowing things to get worse, which they will naturally do without your intervention.

To avoid this tendency, you must simply identify, acknowledge, and resolve the problem. Companies often have trouble with one or more of these steps, which can result in serious litigation.

## IDENTIFYING PROBLEMS

No company has ever solved a problem that it did not know about. It sounds obvious, but you would be surprised at how often a company gets caught completely by surprise when it is served with a civil summons or a criminal subpoena or, worse yet, when it is raided by federal officials looking for evidence of fraud or graft. In a criminal matter or a big civil case, the bad press starts immediately after the suit hits and the company scrambles to put a quick defense together. If the company is on the defensive from the beginning, it becomes more difficult to get the upper hand, and the company is much more likely to agree to an unfavorable settlement—regardless of the facts.

The failure to identify a problem is usually the result of one of the following situations: the company does not train its employees well enough to recognize or correctly report a problem; the company's system of monitoring performance and/or finances does not identify problems quickly enough; or the company fails to monitor the actions or performance of other organizations that impact the company.

### EMPLOYEE TRAINING

In a lot of industries, the rules of the game are counterintuitive. Problems often are not self-evident. Employee training needs to involve more than instruction on how to use the phone system, the way to get direct deposit of paychecks, and how much the company will match retirement contributions. Employees need training about the unique problems that arise in your business and how to handle them. Someone in your company should monitor all of the performance and legal problems that the company has gotten into over the years and work those issues into the training curriculum.

For example, several years ago I represented an investment company that was being sued by a young woman who alleged that she had been fired because of her gender. I interviewed her boss, who had been brought in from a foreign office of the company a few years earlier. I asked him why he had fired the woman. He said that she was not fired because she was a woman, but rather because she intended to get married and have a family within the next year. He said something to the effect of "there's no way we can have a part-timer on this job. I cannot afford to have anybody who is going to be out three months a year, whether it be for maternity leave or anything else."

To him, his reasoning for firing the woman seemed quite acceptable. In his country, the labor laws were very different from those in the United States. He simply did not realize that the reason he cited for not retaining the woman was a flagrant violation of U.S. law and would likely result in a large judgment against the company. Some basic education when he began the job would have avoided the settlement that my client had to pay the woman.

Employment laws are often counterintuitive. Every new employee must therefore be educated about them. Other laws that are counterintuitive include those governing antitrust, government contracts, and product liability. If you have a company that controls a large percentage of the market for your product or service, or that does a lot of business directly or indirectly with the government, or that builds products that can be dangerous to the user, you should invest some time up front rigorously educating your employees on the problems that they might not recognize without some heightened awareness. Spending a little money at the outset for a lawyer might save you a lot in the long run. Most good law firms offer seminars for thirty to forty of your employees on any of these topics for $2,000 to $4,000. Most lawsuits on the same subject will cost you $40,000 to $400,000 or even more—not including whatever settlement or judgment you might have to pay. These seminars are well worth their expense.

Another part of effective employee training is explaining how to report a problem. Employees must feel comfortable speaking frankly, while not getting into the trap of speculating or sending wild and possibly inaccurate e-mails or memos (see mistake number 1 on bad writing, p. 40). There should be a clear means by which to report problems. If the problem is related to performance, company policies should require that the employee report orally to the immediate supervisor, and if there is no action, the employee should report to someone higher up—an open-door policy that normally requires employees to attempt first to speak to their immediate boss.

If the problem involves possibly unethical or criminal conduct, there should be a neutral person in the company who is outside the employee's chain of command, often called an "ombudsman," to whom the employee can and must go to discuss the problem in person, confidentially and without fear of retaliation. By requiring that the employee go to the neutral person, the company will stifle crazy rumors and wild allegations, and, likewise, leave no opportunity for a guilty party to learn of the allegations and cover his or her tracks. Rather, the matter will be thoroughly handled by an appropriately trained person in a professional manner.

## INTERNAL CONTROLS

Often well-trained and highly skilled employees fail to identify problems because the company does not have internal processes that bring problems to light at their earliest stages. Inadequate controls are especially prevalent in systems of financial reporting in medium-sized companies of 50 to 500 employees.

Here is the problem. If a company is spending more money than it had planned to do a job or is paying someone more money than it had planned to for his or her services, there is often little or no way for the company as an entity to realize this problem at the outset. Bills are paid by an accounting person, but reports to those performing the project are either never generated or they are generated well after the expenditure— often weeks or months later. When the project is very expensive, a lag of even a month in financial reporting to project management can unwittingly put a company in a loss position for the duration of the whole project.

A few years ago, I actually witnessed this problem at a very large design and production facility of over 2,500 employees that had fairly sophisticated cost-tracking controls for a major project. The problem at that company was a large number of subdepartments collecting costs, some of which were more conscientious than others at reporting on a regular basis. None of the departments deliberately underreported its costs—ultimately all costs were reported. But some were reported on time, while others were a month late and others two months late. The project was technically difficult and had a challenging schedule, so cost reporting sometimes had to be put on the back burner by some middle managers. Because of the delay in compiling information, unreported costs escalated to the point where they literally formed a growing tidal wave following secretly behind monthly reports that did not look that bad.

## MISTAKE NUMBER 5: IGNORING PROBLEMS

As managers began to run out of money in the budget for their effort long before the work was completed, the financial folks got an escalating number of desperate calls from individual departments. The company, which had been telling its customer that it was on cost and on schedule, had to make the stunning and embarrassing disclosure that it was overrunning so badly that it would go out of business if it did not get some financial relief. What followed was a four-year lawsuit that cost each side over $5 million in legal fees, followed by a resolution that left the customer without the product and the company in financial straits with a tarnished reputation. There is no question that earlier realization of the problem—even three months earlier—would have allowed the parties to restructure the transaction in a far more satisfactory manner.

This same story plays out in nonfinancial contexts. Often, for example, when a company does design work, it does not have adequate testing milestones to determine if its product will be fully functional on time. The company tests the product when it has finished building it, and then realizes that something is wrong with it. Inadequate preproduction testing is another common theme in business litigation.

The solution is real-time financial and performance monitoring. This type of monitoring has never been easier. Many companies have not yet taken full advantage of the amazing leaps in inexpensive computer technology that have hit the market over the past three to five years. For relatively little money, a company that sets financial budgets and performance milestones for all of its work can have its efforts tracked on a daily basis at very little inconvenience to employees, who must do no more than carry out minor daily data entry. A company can know at the end of each day how it is performing on its projects. This kind of tracking is especially easy and inexpensive for small, single-facility companies. When you balance the amount of litigation that can result from improper performance tracking with the minimal cost of good tracking systems, there is no longer any excuse for using antiquated internal control systems. Yet they persist, much to the delight of lawyers.

### MONITORING THIRD PARTIES

For every lawsuit I have seen caused by my own client's failure to identify its problems, I have seen several lawsuits brought about because my client did not realize that a third party upon which it was relying—a customer, a supplier, etc.—had a problem. We discussed earlier the necessity of doing good research on other companies before doing business with them. That process should not stop once the deal has been struck. There should be constant updating of your company's research on its business counterparts.

More important, once you have determined that another company is fit to do business with you, you have an opportunity to define a relationship that will give you even more insight into the workings of that company than you had at the outset. You can, for example, negotiate a contract or make it a condition of a bid that a supplier must give you weekly financial and performance reports. You can include the right of your employees to make on-site visits to monitor performance of any third party that may impact your own performance. In some industries, it is not uncommon for one company to get the right to financial audits of another company.

You might not always be able to negotiate the level of monitoring that you want to have over another company, but there is no harm in trying. If a company wants to do business with you, it may surprise you how far its people are willing to go. If the company is concerned about giving you its proprietary financial data, such as labor rates, or its technical data, you may be able to negotiate confidentiality protections, neutral third-party audits, or other means that protect the proprietary data of your trading counterparts while giving you the performance insight you need to have a lot of confidence that the job will be done on cost and to specifications. Your goal should never be to steal inside data from your competitors or suppliers—that alone can lead to lawsuits. The goal should be to have enough information to ensure that your own business operations will not be adversely impacted by the problems of others.

Another important aspect of third-party performance monitoring is to investigate the *people* with whom you are doing business. As we discussed earlier, it is very easy for companies to change names and personnel. If you experience a problem with a third party, try to determine whether the people at that organization have previously caused you or others problems. Maybe you can solve the problem with a simple change of personnel.

## MISTAKE NUMBER 5: IGNORING PROBLEMS

### ACKNOWLEDGING AND RESOLVING PROBLEMS

Identifying a problem early and defining it coherently are the first steps toward avoiding a lawsuit, but your company will still end up in court if the problem is not effectively *acknowledged* and *resolved*. I have seen a lot of problems go unaddressed in a lot of companies, and there are some recurrent themes. Let's discuss how to resolve the three most common problems that tend to fester without resolution, often resulting in litigation: poor performance by employees, poor performance of a contract, and improper business practices within the company.

### EMPLOYEE PROBLEMS

You may recall when we were discussing "capability speculation" that I came down hard on the supervisor who had speculated that a young broker was ethical and a good manager of accounts, even though the supervisor had never observed the ethics or management practices of the young man. The conclusion was that you should never speculate about a personal quality of another but only comment based on actual observation.

Well, the problem can get worse. Often, speculation degenerates into misrepresentation. There is a pervasive problem in the corporate world with supervisors knowingly making misstatements on employee evaluation forms. Just as there is now notorious grade inflation in American high schools and colleges, corporations have an equally notorious, litigation-fanning practice of giving employees good performance evaluations when they do not deserve them—even where there is direct observation by a supervisor to the contrary.

A company has to learn to stand up and correct employee problems—laziness, incompetence, prejudice, lack of team spirit, and the like. Recently, I had the "opportunity" to work with a thoroughly incompetent accountant at a medium-sized company. I felt sorry for the guy, who was clearly in the wrong profession. He tried in vain to help me calculate the damages that the company had sustained as the result of a breach of contract by another organization. The amount in controversy was roughly $300,000, and the matter involved no complex financial issues. Eventually, I had to make the calculations myself, which I did successfully, and I am no math wizard.

95

It so happened that about a year later, the accountant was laid off from the company as part of an unfortunate 10 percent downsizing initiative. The bad accountant was laid off because his supervisor determined that he was the least capable accountant in the ten-person department. The accountant promptly sued for age discrimination. My firm represented the company, and I recall telling the lawyer in my firm who was handling the case that she had a slam dunk of a case on her hands because this guy was, frankly, incompetent. It was obvious to me from personal experience that age had nothing to do with the layoff.

The lawyer in my firm invited me into her office and pulled out a few sheets of paper from a folder. "Look at these," she said. The papers were the performance evaluations for the accountant: SPEED—good; ACCURACY—good; WILLINGNESS TO WORK HARD—good, they read, and the list went on. It turns out that this was in fact the *worst* evaluation that had been given to any of the company's ten accountants. Most of the other accountants had some "excellents" as well as "goods" in their evaluations, but the complete failure of the company to say even one bad thing about this incompetent guy made the company's case a lot harder to win.

> Company supervisors are doing a disservice to everyone except trial lawyers when they are disingenuous in their evaluations of those working for them. An unwarranted positive evaluation discourages improvement. Moreover, taking the easy way out by not acknowledging a problem up front will often cause it to resurface much more dangerously in litigation.

Not only do supervisors need to be more honest in their critiques, but they also must provide clear examples to support a negative evaluation. Even in the relatively few cases in which I have seen supervisors give a "fair" or "poor" evaluation to an employee, the supervisor often does not fill out the part of the form that allows for comments—usually because he or she had "higher priorities" (e.g., laziness). Once the employee is gone and the lawsuit hits, the lawyer for the former employee notes the lack of comments on the evaluation sheet and asks the jury to infer that there was some ulterior motive for the bad evaluation. If, however, there are clear, concrete examples of poor performance documented at the time of the evaluation, the company has made itself effectively suitproof.

Honest evaluations will greatly protect the company from unmeritorious lawsuits by former employees bent on getting back at the company. But do not forget that the company can be equally burned by giving an honestly bad evaluation and then not doing anything about it. For example, I recall a case in which a tour director at a travel company had received bad evaluations, but the company continued to give that employee major responsibilities. He ended up badly botching a big Caribbean golf outing and got the tour company sued for about $90,000. The other side got hold of the evaluations during the litigation discovery process and forced the travel company into a very unfavorable $70,000 settlement because everyone knew that a jury would nail the company for keeping an employee with such a bad performance history.

It sounds so simple, but it is so rarely practiced. Be honest in your evaluations, and act on your criticism. If you're too nice, you could be scathed by the employee later on; if you're honest but do nothing to correct a problem, you have exposed the company to liability to third parties. It happens every day.

## CRITICAL PATH ANALYSIS

As you have seen, ignoring problems with your own employees causes lawsuits. One corporate attorney at a Fortune 500 company recently told me that she had seventy-five ex-employee lawsuits going on at any given time, most of which could have been avoided had the employees been honestly evaluated. But she also told me that the total amount of money in controversy in the seventy-five employment suits was less than the amount in controversy in the five breach of contract suits that the company had going on with its subcontractors and customers.

As bad as internal problems can be, ignoring problems with your company's customers and suppliers often exposes the company to much greater liability. As we touched on earlier, the biggest business lawsuits result when either a supplier cannot technically or financially complete a job or when a customer does not accurately define its needs. The result is either an ineffective product or an effective product that is delivered too late to do much good.

Of course, it is not uncommon for suppliers to have technical difficulties, and most customers redefine their needs during the course of a job. Products or services are often late or imperfect, and it is often no big deal. The serious legal exposure comes when the problems reach what is known as the "critical path." A problem hits the critical path when it causes a chain reaction of other problems, putting the entire project in jeopardy. Management consultants often call this process the "ripple effect." While it is always a good idea to address a problem immediately, it is unrealistic to expect that this will occur every time. If you adopt a more modest goal of avoiding costly litigation, the rule to follow is to address a problem before it hits the "critical path."

Every employee needs to understand the basics of critical path analysis. Here is an example from real life (altered to protect the innocent). A company designs a winter weather ice-monitoring system that goes on airport runways. The local aviation authorities require such a system to be operational during the winter months for any airport. A city hires that company to design such a system for its new airport. The contract calls for the delivery and installation of the winter weather monitoring system to be completed by April 1, 1999. The airport is scheduled to be opened four months later, on August 1, 1999, and all the airlines have started booking flights into the airport on the assumption of an August 1 opening.

Then the problem hits. It is not important whether the problem is the fault of the city or the company. The airport could have changed its runway temperature sensitivity requirements in the middle of the design process, or the company could have run into technical difficulty getting accurate temperature readings due to an unusual runway design. Either way, there is a problem.

Should the company just continue to work and worry about financial and/or scope-of-work relief later, or should it get together with the airport authority and try to work out a schedule change or technical modification to the contract right away? Here is where critical path analysis comes in. The company must immediately determine whether it can afford to complete the job without immediate financial relief. If it cannot, then the company will stop work. The airport authority faces the prospect of an airport that cannot open until it hires a totally new company to complete the job many months later. That in turn means airlines will not be able to service their customers as they have promised, business travelers will miss appointments, and so on—a ripple effect. If the company cannot complete the job, the problem is on the airport's critical path. This is a basic example of a critical path problem that both parties must resolve immediately.

Most cases are not that simple. Assume, for example, that the weather system company can *financially* afford to resolve the problem and complete the job. The company must then determine the impact the problem will have on the schedule. Suppose the problem will delay the installation of the weather system by two to five months. The weather system completion date will move from April 1 to June 1 at the earliest. At first glance, it does not look like a critical path problem because the airport is not supposed to open until August 1, and the job will probably be completed by June 1—two months before the airport opens. Moreover, the company may rationalize that even if the problem ends up taking an extra five months (until September 1), the airport can still open on August 1 because it does not need the winter weather system when the airport opens in August. So the company decides it is okay to give the airport authority an operational weather system two to five months late. The problem does not appear to be on the critical path because it does not have a ripple effect, right?

Wrong. There is another company in the picture: the runway asphalt sealing contractor. The sealing company needs to have the weather system installed before it does any sealing, and the runway *has* to be sealed before *any* plane lands. The sealing takes three months and it was supposed to have started on April 1, the day that the weather system installation was to have been completed. Thus, even a two-month delay on the weather system pushes the sealing completion ahead from July 1 to September 1. The airport can no longer open on time on August 1. The mere two-month delay by the weather system company is on the critical path because it pushes the sealing completion to after the August 1 opening date.

That is a rudimentary critical path analysis. Employees must appreciate the importance of the critical path. Bosses, customers, and suppliers may rant and rave about a problem or a delay, but such setbacks do not usually incur enough damages to justify going to court unless the problem impacts the critical path. Consequently, critical path analysis must become second nature to all responsible employees. Try to address all problems, and most importantly never let one hit the critical path.

## Conspiracy Theory

I have saved the worst for last. Companies tend to let moral and ethical problems fester the longest, yet these problems, if left unaddressed, have the most severe ramifications for the company. I asked some business acquaintances at several larger companies what kinds of ethical allegations they most commonly hear. Aside from petty office theft, which was the overwhelming problem, the following are four of the most common ethical situations that come up in companies: an employee reports that another employee took an expensive gift or bribe from a subcontractor; an employee claims that a supervisor submitted an inflated claim for payment to an insurance company or to the federal government; an employee states that a company officer engaged in insider trading; and an employee says that he or she was directed due to budget problems to charge time to a job that he or she was not working on.

These are all very serious allegations. If true, a person who committed any of these offenses could suffer serious legal consequences. Many companies are numbed into inaction when the allegations surface. They simply do not know what to do. Some do nothing; others may authorize a cursory investigation, but they often really do not want to hear the outcome unless it is positive. When you do nothing or not enough, you can turn a civil case into a criminal one, or you can turn a criminal case with weak grounds into one with strong evidence.

Let's use the example of an inflated claim, although the logic holds for all four situations mentioned above. Say that your company sells and installs carpet at the Department of Education in Washington. A brand-new company accountant, John Billman, submits an invoice to the education department that reads:

FOR CARPET SERVICES RENDERED:

| | |
|---|---|
| Material: | $ 2,500 |
| Labor: | $ 4,800 |
| Travel: (est.) | $ 5,400 |
| Total: | $ 12,700 |

## MISTAKE NUMBER 5: IGNORING PROBLEMS

The government accounts receivable employee reviews the bill and finds that the travel cost, which exceeds both the labor and the material, is exorbitant. He sends an auditor to your company to look at the books. The auditor finds that the actual travel costs were $890, not the $5,400 submitted. The auditors immediately notify federal investigators. The investigators show up at the company unannounced (as they are trained to do) and demand to speak to the young Mr. Billman. He is terrified and quite sincerely says that the $5,400 was an estimate, as indicated on the bill, because the actual travel vouchers were not available at the time he prepared the bill. "You see," he says, "immediately after the Department of Education job, the laborers went overseas for six more months on another job, so I had no travel vouchers." Billman further states that he used $5,400 as the travel estimate because that was the travel expense on the previous job for the same customer. It seemed comparable. The federal investigators then ask Billman if he knew that the previous job involved over four times as much material and labor—hence a lot more travel cost. "Oops," says Mr. Billman, "I made a bad estimate."

All right. Billman is an idiot, but he is not a criminal. He made a mistake and subjected his company to civil liability for a negligently false claim probably amounting to the difference between $890 and $5,400 ($4,510), plus a penalty. The reason there is no basis for a criminal case is that there was no *intentional* misconduct. No one meant to harm the government, so no one is going to jail; there should be no bad press or scandal.

The situation could have a different ending. The government investigators do not just interview people, they also come armed with subpoenas for documents relating to the transaction at issue. They get the documents. In this case, two documents catch their eyes. One is a memo from Billman's billing supervisor to the vice president of finance, attached to the bill with the $5,400 travel estimate on it, with a one-line note: "What, did these guys fly on the Concorde?"

A civil case just became a criminal case. It is obvious from the note that, while Billman was unaware of his mistake, his supervisor knew that the travel cost was probably wrong. So the element of *intent* is now arguably present. At a minimum, what was formerly a negligent false claim may now have become a "knowing" false claim. The investigator will tell the prosecutor that the supervisor knew that the government was being cheated. So even though the underlying act was not criminal, a company executive's conscious decision not to address the problem might have been.

Even so, it is still not a very strong criminal case because the supervisor made a rather passive comment. But all too typically, here is how the situation worsens. The busy vice president of finance sends the note back to the supervisor with his own seemingly innocuous one-liner: "Don't worry about it." In other words, ignore the problem.

Now what started as a civil case and then became a weak criminal case has now become a good criminal case. Why? A senior official has sanctioned conduct that he seems to know involved an inflated bill to the government. People have gone to jail for less.

In fact, in the great political scandals of the past twenty-five years, the majority of those who went to jail had not committed an "underlying" offense. Consider Watergate, the Iran-Contra affair, the savings and loan scandal, or even the more recent Travelgate, Whitewater, fund-raising, and other presidential scandals. Few people were punished for the Watergate break-in, or for the diversion of arms to Iran, or for bilking the public of its savings. Rather the majority were accused or jailed for cover-ups, obstruction of justice, aiding and abetting, or conspiracies. In each situation, the prosecution lacked a good case until someone deliberately ignored or intentionally hid a problem.

Cover-ups are most desirable to prosecutors because, by definition, they involve actions more recent in time than the underlying event being covered up and by nature tend to involve higher-level officials. Cover-ups also tend to involve fewer witnesses and documents, thereby allowing prosecutors to steer clear of the more complicated underlying transactions. Equally important, prosecutors know that juries are quick to infer criminal intent when they see evidence of a cover-up.

All that misery—the literal destruction of corporate and personal lives—because of a few careless words reflecting the intent to hide a known problem. Ignoring a problem is the best way to turn a minor civil liability into a major criminal one. It happens to good people. It can happen to you.

# MISTAKE NUMBER 6:
# GETTING PERSONAL

## CORPORATION: PERSON OR MACHINE?

Another sure route to the courthouse is a business dispute that gets personal. The question of how much emotion is appropriate in the workplace goes to the very nature and purpose of a corporate legal structure.

Traditionally defined, a corporation is a legal entity formed to transact business in a manner delineated by state law, which includes the ability to make contracts and limited personal liability for those acting on the corporation's behalf. However, one of the first lessons a law student learns is that a corporation is also a fictional "person." Like people, corporations have a birth and a life; they grow; they do business; they can commit crimes; they can sue and be sued; they can fail; they die. Law students are often taught to imagine a company as a living being, complete with its own corporate attitude and personality. In learning about "client relations," students are encouraged to understand differing corporate cultures just as they would endeavor to understand different human cultures.

Economists and business people may tell you, however, that a *successful* corporation is really more like a machine than a person. The purpose of a corporation is to take raw elements—ideas, motivation, labor, and materials—and assemble them in a manner that creates a profitable product or service. Corporate success requires an efficient, carefully calculated assault on the marketplace. It is almost a scientific process. Emotion can only skew this process.

The truth is that a successful corporation is probably somewhere in between a person and a machine. Even the most rigid corporate executives know that there is room in the machine for a limited amount of human emotion: pride in the product, a synergistic spirit of mission among employees. Indeed, these emotions are often the difference between corporations that merely survive and those that truly thrive. Part of what makes a successful company greater than the sum of its parts is the spirit of the people working together toward corporate objectives.

But the company only has room for emotions that reflect overall corporate goals. Individual agendas—prejudices, personality conflicts, hostility rooted outside the workplace—all distort the near-mechanical process of producing a product or service that will compete effectively in the marketplace. It's like putting gum in a gearbox.

A lot of business lawsuits result from emotion gone awry. As we have seen in previous examples, sometimes a legal problem develops from within the company, and other times it results from conflicts between companies. But whether it is an issue between an employer and employee or between companies, the role that emotion plays is really no different: lawsuits arise when individual emotions get in the way of corporate goals.

We will first talk about intracompany emotional problems and then move to intercompany personality conflicts.

## THE HOSTILE ENVIRONMENT

### PREJUDICE

Prejudice has historically been the biggest emotional problem within companies. There is no denying it. For decades, corporations were the bastions of white males. As women and minorities began to push for their rights, it became evident that antidiscrimination laws were necessary.

In the early days of corporate reform, about 1970 to 1980, the law held a company liable for discrimination on the basis of sex, race, religion, or age when there was concrete evidence that someone in the company was refusing to hire, promote, or retain an employee on the basis of a personal quality unrelated to competence. The line of prejudice was pretty clear, and it was often crossed. Employees brought successful suits when they proved that supervisors used overt racial slurs or demanded that their employees sleep with them, or when a woman had been refused employment because, as one supervisor remarked, "she was Catholic, just married, and I couldn't afford an accountant off on maternity leave every 10 months." These were clear cases of discrimination not only under federal guidelines but also according to the basic moral principles shared by most Americans.

Over the years, companies began training their employees only to make decisions based on performance. They learned clear rules governing sexual harassment and racial discrimination. Some companies believed that they could change people's prejudices with sensitivity training. Others assumed perhaps more realistically that they could educate their employees using immediate termination as the consequence of discrimination.

These programs had significant, albeit incomplete, success. To a large extent, companies have rooted out overt discrimination. There have, of course, been notable exceptions in recent years, such as the Texaco fiasco of 1996, in which top management was recorded making racially insensitive remarks; but when the facts came out fully, even that incident was mild compared to the ingrained corporate prejudices evident in cases fifteen or twenty years earlier.

However, as overtly ignorant ogres left the corporate scene, they were replaced by a smaller crop of slightly more polished corporate managers who harbored the same prejudices but expressed them in a more subtle manner. Employees started filing suits recognized by courts for a "hostile environment." Employees claimed a right of action even when there had been no overt act of discrimination or harassment. Rather they complained of an overall environment that was not conducive to women, minorities, older employees, etc. The courts agreed that there was a legitimate basis for a suit under such circumstances.

For example, while writing this book, I learned of a case in which seven or eight male employees who worked under a particular supervisor had a "video club." Each Monday morning, they would bring X-rated videos to work and trade them. There were no movies shown on the corporate premises, but the mere existence of the "club" made the two women in the department very uncomfortable. Not only did they feel degraded, they said they also resented any "club" that by definition excluded them. They threatened to sue for a "hostile environment," and the "club" was disbanded. This was exactly the type of situation that the courts envisioned could create sexual harassment without an overt act perpetrated directly against one of the women. It was a work environment that was hostile and unflattering to women.

However, in recent years the "hostile environment" and related legal standards for determining discrimination have developed a problem: their limits are impossible to grasp. Take, for example, a case in which a company supervisor held his twice-annual retreat at a lake where everyone went water-skiing. Three older employees said they did not go to the lake because they were not in any condition to water-ski. Did that supervisor create an environment hostile to older people? The older employees felt as if they were outcasts and that it hurt their overall position in the company.

Another case involved a minority employee who regularly and without authorization took a company vehicle to run personal errands, in direct violation of an explicit company policy. The employee was reprimanded and later fired. The employee sued on the grounds that her civil rights had been violated because the supervisor had on a few occasions let a white employee use the vehicle for personal reasons without repercussions. The lawyer for the fired employee argued that allowing one employee to breach company policy while reprimanding a minority for doing the same created actionable racial discrimination.

Companies spend millions of dollars trying to explain to their employees which actions will constitute a hostile environment or other violations of employment law. It is an impossible task because lawyers and judges do not even know. Before we discuss a more practical solution, let's first explore misconduct outside of prejudice, and see if we cannot come up with a universal and understandable standard of conduct.

## BUSINESS ETHICS

The problem of a nebulous standard of proper personal corporate conduct is not limited to discrimination and harassment cases. There is also the problem of the employee who reports legal or ethical misconduct—the whistle-blower. In the old days, we saw clear-cut cases, in which, for example, an employee reported a bribe and the supervisor fired him or her. Clearly, this situation involved an improper retaliatory discharge of the employee who had reported misconduct. As in the early prejudice cases, there was no question that something had to be done to protect the victimized employee. So laws were passed giving all kinds of protection to whistle-blowers, amounting to virtual job security. Some of the laws even gave whistle-blowers a percentage of any money recovered by the government as a result of revealing corporate misconduct.

However, with job security and cash as incentives, a lot of whistle-blower cases arose in which it was unclear whether a corporate wrong had been committed or whether a lazy and/or vindictive employee just wanted to get back at someone, get some job security, or cash in. For example, under one whistle-blower law known as the False Claims Act, the government evaluates the merit of whistle-blower suits to determine if it wants to take part. It declines in over 75 percent of the cases filed, implying that such cases may not be valid.

Consequently, today it is often very hard to tell if an employee is just disgruntled and frustrated or if there is a real problem at the company. I have seen many cases in which the company hired outsiders to investigate the reportedly improper incident, and the independent investigation revealed nothing more than a personality conflict between an employee and his or her supervisor. But the law now provides so much protection for whistle-blowers that he or she has a lot of incentive to be as vocal, outlandish, and disruptive as possible. It seems that the more he or she complains, the less the company can do about it. So many companies are left with the choice of struggling dysfunctionally with counterproductive employees or firing them and getting sued.

## THE MARKET-EFFECT RESOLUTION

Whether workplaces constitute actionably "hostile environments" and whether whistle-blowers are legitimate have become sticky legal issues for lawyers and the courts to resolve. If lawyers and judges cannot resolve the issues, it is impossible to expect a company to educate its employees on the appropriate standard of legal conduct. Consequently, corporations must adopt a standard of conduct so clearly acceptable that it takes into account any possible legal liability. That means employees must do more than avoid overt discrimination and harassment. They must do more than just try to avoid a hostile environment, whatever that is. They must do more than agree to refrain from retaliating against "troublemakers." But what, then, is the appropriate standard of conduct?

There is a clear solution. It involves swinging back a bit toward the perception of the corporation as a "machine" rather than a "person." The solution is to adopt a market-based standard of conduct rather than a moral or law-based standard. That means that, in evaluating the propriety of their actions, employees and their supervisors must ask themselves if their personal attitude, demeanor, or situation is interfering with the company goal of providing a high-quality product or service at a price that is competitive. If there is such interference, the company should require immediate corrective action.

For example, if two people in the department are not talking to each other because of a personality, racial, or some other conflict, there is a communication gap that by definition adversely affects productivity. The underlying issue that got them to stop communicating, therefore, involved inappropriate corporate conduct. Unless there was criminal conduct that the company must report to authorities, it does not matter whether there really was an ethically inappropriate action or not. Who is "right" and who is "wrong" is irrelevant to the corporate goal. It is the duty of the company to resolve the problem so that the inefficiency is eliminated. The employees do not have to "make up"; they do not have to like each other. But they do have to develop a market-efficient solution. That might mean something as simple as a truce. It might mean an agreement to refrain from certain conduct with or without an admission that such conduct was wrong. It might require an office move, or it might require reshuffling of some responsibilities or redefining the interaction between personnel. Whatever the solution, the company policy must be clear: it will not tolerate employees who let their personal, emotional, or social situation interfere with the corporate goal of winning in the marketplace. Employees should understand from the moment that they begin at the company that any prolonged distraction, illegal or otherwise, from the corporate objective will result in *termination* of all parties involved.

At first glance, this somewhat cold, market-focused solution to personal issues in the workplace seems to run contrary to the literal tidal wave of ethics training that companies have embraced in the past six to eight years. In seeking to avoid discrimination and ethics-based lawsuits, companies presently tend to emphasize the human aspects of corporate life more than the business aspects. "Take the High Road" is a wonderful booklet used by one of my clients to educate employees on issues of business ethics, and I would encourage all companies to provide such training.

But if you are trying to avoid lawsuits, the standard needs to be broader, clearer, and more objective. Whether the problem is ethical or unethical, as a corporate employee, you must correct conduct that is interfering with corporate goals. Indeed, the reason that using the bottom line to guide you is consistent with ethical resolutions is that the market approach literally subsumes the ethical one. If a personal problem in the workplace is resolved by considering how it is affecting business, the personal and ethical issues will evaporate. The market approach includes all ethical problems, but it also includes all other problems that interfere with the corporate goals of your company. You must refrain from all conduct that reduces corporate efficiency.

## THE FICTIONAL DEMON

As we discussed above, companies start out as a fiction, a figment of the imagination. Some say they become machines. To others, they become living, breathing persons. But in a lawsuit, your corporate opponent becomes Satan himself! Indeed, the demonization of the other guy is not only a frequent cause of lawsuits, it also can ultimately result in a hefty judgment or settlement coming out of your corporate cash reserves. Let's spend some time analyzing the risks of getting personal with the other side.

### CHANGING STANDARDS

By now you should have no doubt that one principal reason for the recent litigation explosion is that the standards of proper conduct are so hard to define. We have already covered the difficulty in separating civil from criminal misconduct, discrimination from insensitivity, ethical uprightness from personal vendettas.

In terms of "getting personal" with other companies, the risk again lies in changing and ill-defined standards. The risk of personal assaults against another company is that a run-of-the-mill contract action will burgeon into the more serious "tort" actions we touched on earlier.

Let's analyze the difference between a contract and a tort action in greater depth.

Most business relationships are defined by a contractual document. The relationship may be classified as a sale, a lease, a trust, a mortgage, a prime contract, a licensing agreement, a merger agreement, an agency agreement, a sponsorship agreement, a loan, or a guarantee. All of these agreements, among others, are contracts.

For many years, the usual remedy for breach of any contractual agreement was the out-of-pocket loss of the injured party, plus reasonably proven lost profits, if any. For example, suppose that you agree to provide me with 1,000 pounds of table-grade particle board at $10 per pound so that I can build 100 tables and sell them to Denny's at a $30 per-table profit. You do not deliver the particle board. I rush out and buy particle board elsewhere at a pricey $12 per pound, and, due to your delay, I only have enough time to build 90 of the 100 tables. You have breached your contract with me. I have a contract action against you for the increased cost of the lumber: $12 per pound minus $10 per pound times 1,000 pounds, for a total of $2,000 in out-of-pocket losses. And I also might be able to recover from you my lost profits on the tables I could not build because of your delay: the 100 tables contracted minus 90 tables I built times $30 profit per table, for a total lost profit of $300. Total damages would equal $2,000 plus $300 or $2,300.

Over the past twenty-five years, the laws governing business contracts have slid into the murky world of "torts." Traditionally, torts are actions for injury due to negligent or intentional misconduct. For example, a person who falls in the lobby of your office because of a wet floor has a tort action rooted in your negligence. The settlements of "negligent torts" not only reward the plaintiff with money for out-of-pocket damages such as medical bills and lost "profits" such as wages *but also for pain and suffering*.

Then come the "intentional torts." Hitting someone over the head was the typical intentional tort. The remedy for such a deliberate act of misconduct was not only out-of-pocket damages, lost profits or wages, and restitution for pain and suffering, but also *punitive* damages. The jury could award the victim money—and often lots of it—just to punish the other side. Until recent legal reforms, it was not unheard of to see a verdict of $10,000 for out-of-pocket losses, $100,000 for lost wages, $500,000 for pain and suffering, and $10 million for punitive damages.

## MISTAKE NUMBER 6: GETTING PERSONAL

The money still lies in proving that the other side's actions were intentionally harmful so you can get punitive damages. You may recall my earlier discussion of the case in which a company's alleged decision to estimate the value of a life turned a *negligent* tort into an *intentional* tort. There is a tremendous financial incentive for a plaintiff's attorney to transform a negligent tort into an intentional tort whenever legally possible.

In business contracts litigation, the money is in making the even bigger jump from a traditional breach of contract to conspiracies and intentional torts. Historically, the most viable actions for intentional misconduct in connection with business transactions were antitrust and fraud cases. Antitrust violations included conspiracies by powerful companies to drive others out of business through price fixing and other schemes. Tort actions for fraud most often involved getting a party to sign a contract on the basis of false representations. In the case of antitrust violations, the offending company had to pay triple damages or more. In the case of fraudulent inducement, the injured party got out of the contract and sometimes received punitive damages. The rules for training employees were as follows: do not conspire to destroy the competition and do not get the other side to sign a contract by lying to them. The lines were relatively clear.

No longer. Over the past several decades, courts have recognized increasingly nebulous claims arising from the performance of business contracts. The courts have allowed companies to claim punitive damages for what are at best traditional breaches of contract. The injured party now tacks on allegations of an improper motive underlying the breach. These torts go by a variety of old names with expanded applications: unfair competition, tortious interference with a business relationship, tortious interference with a business expectation, among others.

A new, and by far the scariest, business tort is the *prima facie* tort by which you can be held liable for a *legal* action taken for an "improper" purpose. The oft-used hypothetical example of a *prima facie* tort is the case in which a bank forecloses on a mortgage in accordance with the terms of the mortgage but is still held liable for punitive damages. Why? Because the loan officer knew when he foreclosed that the mortgagee had just inherited some money that would be released from probate only two days later. The mortgagee proves that the bank foreclosed on the first possible day because the loan officer and the mortgagee's wife were rivals running for the school board and the bank officer wanted to embarrass the mortgagee. So a lawful action, a foreclosure in accordance with the terms of the mortgage, becomes the basis for a punitive damages claim.

The bizarre developments in tort law mean that a traditional small-dollar contract dispute can now be easily transformed into a big-dollar tort action if the other side can allege (not necessarily even prove) that the actions you took were for improper purposes. Lawsuits that once were not worth the filing fees now look quite promising to companies, egged on by their lawyers' promises of big punitive damages awards.

These developments mean that the more personal you get in your dislike of another company or its employees, the more likely you are to give them the basis to file a high-dollar tort suit against your company due to your allegedly "malicious" or "intentional" acts. The suit may be ridiculous and unfounded, but, as we know, the courts are often too busy to sift through cases early on, so you are likely to have to prepare a costly defense against such allegations.

For example, I recently represented a subcontractor that was sued by the prime for breach of subcontract. There was about a million dollars at stake, and it was a pretty low-key case—that is until we had to produce the personal notebook and memos of my client's contract administrator. It turned out that our guy hated his counterpart at the prime contractor so much that he had written a memo to our management and recommended that our company go directly to the customer and tell them how bad this other person was. The contract administrator hoped that the customer would never allow the other guy to work on another prime contract again. Our company categorically rejected the suggestion, but the memos and notes containing the suggestion survived. As soon as the other side got hold of the notes, its lawyers amended the suit to claim $15 million in lost business from the customer due to the allegedly tortious actions of my client and they wanted another $15 million in punitive damages as well. The fact remained that my client, the subcontractor, had never communicated directly with the customer and the customer had stopped doing business with the prime in part because the prime employee in question really was impossible. So, although the subcontractor was right, it didn't matter. As soon as the other side had evidence that the matter had gotten personal, a big tort action was born.

## MISTAKE NUMBER 6: GETTING PERSONAL

### TORTIOUS EVIDENCE

We will assume for the purposes of the discussion below that your company has not actually engaged in any sort of tortious conspiracy against the other side. The following are the kinds of emotional behavior that, even if your actions were legally acceptable, can turn minor contract disputes into big tort lawsuits:

(a) *Making gratuitously insulting remarks about the competition:* There is no problem with saying that your product tests, sells, or performs better than that of the competition. That's business. But juries do not like bullies. If you speak or write to customers, or even write internal memos using disparaging remarks about the competition, you are opening yourself up to allegations of tortious interference with business relationships. I once heard allegations that a senior corporate executive had remarked at a meeting, in sick humor, that his goal was for the children of the employees of the competition to starve. Very funny, but it was soon all over the newspapers, resulting in tremendous pressure on the company to come up with a cash settlement. More important, I have seen companies get into trouble by calling the competition such seemingly innocuous names as "losers," "small potatoes," and even "a bunch of clowns." These statements have no substance; they add no value and they can cost you a lot. Don't use them.

(b) *Trying to get someone at another company fired:* I know of several instances in which companies were hurt when their people had a meeting and decided it was their mission to get rid of someone at another company. If there is a problem with an individual employee at another company, you should handle the matter by having a single high-level person at your company communicate professionally with a similarly situated person at the other company. No plans, no plots. High-level diplomacy is much better than low-brow backstabbing.

(c) *Writing histrionic letters:* We touched on this issue in the "Bad Writing" section, but it is worthy of some elaboration. As a business dispute progresses, a letter-writing campaign begins. Each party gets some sort of therapeutic release from concocting replies that are dripping with unnecessary adjectives such as "outrageous," "preposterous," "ridiculous," and "ludicrous." No doubt you've seen such responses. These kinds of letters are actually quite fun to write. As I mentioned before, lawyers write them all the time, and it is usually a harmless (although not helpful) practice because letters from lawyers do not often become evidence at a trial. For business people, however, such letters can be harmful. When the dust settles and you are deciding the merits of your case, it is usually the party that remained totally professional in tone that comes out ahead. If you don't use nasty words, your letter will have a powerful persuasiveness based on fact and reason, in contrast to the emotional irrationality of the other side.

(d) *Using profanity or sexual references:* A jury will infer evil motives to anyone with a foul or offensive demeanor. I worked on a case in which my client was accused of unfair competition. The other company claimed that one of my witnesses had had secret meetings with the government of Thailand in which he conspired to destroy the business relationship between the other company and the Thai government. None of these alleged meetings actually had occurred. However, our witness's personal diaries, oral statements, and memos to his team were full of bad language and profane references to the effect that "we do what's in the contract and nuthin f***ing more," and "watch out everyone, they're gonna slip it to us." During his deposition, he was grilled on these statements, and it was easy for the other side to make him look like an untrustworthy sleazebag. Fortunately, the other side had a couple of guys who were even worse than he was, so the case was settled favorably for my client.

Try to keep in mind that everything you say or write might come back to you in a public proceeding, in which your actions will be evaluated by retired schoolteachers, the local florist, homemakers, and the other people who make up a jury of your peers. They usually want to side with the nice guy, and they are more inclined to believe in tortious conspiracies and devious intent on the part of witnesses whom they just do not like. I even recommend that you refrain from the quite popular practice of using nicknames when describing employees in other organizations—"Ratbag Willie," "Johnny Red-nose," and "Dave the Snake" appeared in memos I read recently. They provide some mild humor at work but are not worth the risk of prompting a retired schoolteacher on a jury to award punitive damages against your company. Jokes about lawyers are, however, usually okay. They offend no one.

## THE SAVIOR

One last note about getting personal with the other side. Sometimes liability results from being too *nice* to the other side, believe it or not. When a company encounters some internal problems in the performance of a job for a customer, it is not uncommon for the company to replace the personnel who were working on the job with some fresh faces. Sometimes the outgoing people in the company are quite resentful of the new group that the company has called in to save the day. There can be some real friction within the company as the old and new teams must work together to pass the torch to the new people.

Often the new personnel, almost as an outlet for the tension they are experiencing within their own company, will introduce themselves to the customer by apologizing profusely for the poor performance of the previous company team. As an effort to assure the customer that the project will be well run from here on out, the new people will badmouth the technical or management abilities of their fellow employees who preceded them on the job. I have even seen employees apologize in writing for the performance of their predecessors.

This practice is always counterproductive. If current employees admit to third parties that co-workers previously screwed things up, they might as well just write a check to the other side for any conceivable loss that the other side might try to pin on them at some later time. It is not the job of the new team to disparage the old one. Half the time the new employees do not really even know how much the first employees are to blame for problems, but they apologize nonetheless. Falling on your sword never gets a job done. Just go in and do a better job.

# MISTAKE NUMBER 7:
# SIDE DEALS

It seems that everyone these days has to be running his or her own side show. Whether it's a development contract, a sales contract, a joint venture, or a licensing agreement, someone thinks that he or she understands the deal better than the people who negotiated it and wrote it down. So individuals take matters into their own hands and end up costing the company a fortune.

A lot of the problems described in this section arise from poorly written contracts and could have been discussed in the earlier section on bad writing. What differentiates the following section from the bad writing section is that this section does not deal with the style or form of written documents, but rather with the way in which the contract language can pave the way for extracontractual misunderstandings.

### THE "FOUR CORNERS" DOCTRINE

In the legal world, paper used to be stronger than iron. Having something on paper not only protected you from the contrary allegations of the other side but it also protected you from yourself. Courts just did not allow an ill-advised statement made by an ignorant employee on either side to alter the deal as it had been written.

This is no longer the case. You have to be prepared to have the jury hear anything you have said, you think you possibly said, you meant to say, you implied, you would have said if you had remembered to say it, or for that matter, anything you dreamt when you were four years old. It seems that in at least half of the lawsuits that I handle, someone is arguing that what the deal *says* and what the deal *is* are two different things. Unfortunately, therefore, believing that the language of the contract gives you absolute protection against actions based on side deals is another big cause of lawsuits.

In the old days, courts ruled that contracts were governed by their "four corners." That meant that you looked at the totality of the written contract to determine its meaning, and also that the deal was defined on the paper and nowhere else. There were three common law or statutory legal protections that precluded lawsuits based on side deals—the parole evidence rule, the integration rule, and the statute of frauds. The rules were simple. The parole evidence rule said that the written deal is *the* deal and that precontract negotiations are irrelevant and not even admissible in court. The integration rule meant that we could assume that the written deal covered all issues related to the deal. The statute of frauds stated that a wide variety of oral deals—normally oral commitments that would take a year or longer to perform—were not legally enforceable. The drafters of contracts then closed any loopholes in these rules by putting clauses in the agreement to the effect that the agreement could not be orally modified. *Voilà!* The perfect written contract.

## A TEAR IN THE PAPER

There are and always have been exceptions to the rule that the written deal is *the* deal even when the contract expressly precludes oral modifications. The difference between the way things once were and the way they are now is that courts today are much more willing to allow a party to present exceptions to a jury. In the past, courts often granted motions to dismiss cases or to issue a judgment without trial when one side had proved that the other side had made an argument inconsistent with the express terms of the contract. The judicial practice of quickly stopping cases in which one side said the contract didn't mean what it said discouraged companies from filing such cases.

Nowadays, judges do not have as much time to hear arguments or write opinions preventing exceptions to the "four corners rule." If one side in a lawsuit makes the mere allegation that an exception to the "four corners rule" applies, that may be the end of the issue until the jury decides the matter. Companies, therefore, have no qualms about filing suits alleging all kinds of agreements that are absolutely antithetical to the language of the contract.

Here are some of the ever-expanding exceptions to the "four corners rule."

## "CLEAR" AMBIGUITY

The courts have always held that if language in an agreement is susceptible to multiple meanings, the parties may use negotiation notes, personal recollection, or industry practice to clarify the ambiguous phrases. For example, if the contract says I will provide you with "commercial-grade" silicon, and we disagree with each other on how much impurity is permissible in commercial-grade silicon, then we can pull out negotiation notes or a chemical handbook that says commercial grade means 98 percent pure. Such an exception is understandable. Side discussions of this kind are admissible to illuminate unclear phrases.

The problem is that now parties get away with alleging that almost anything is ambiguous so that the exception has become the rule. Courts often find ambiguity in seemingly clear phrases if someone so much as alleges a side deal. For example, I know of a case in which a contract (which stated that it could only be modified in writing) contained a provision to the effect that a company had the "sole, exclusive, and unreviewable right to select its employees for the job." During the performance of the contract, the other side complained about one employee and allegedly got an oral agreement to have him removed from the job. When the employee was not removed, the other side terminated the contract for default and sued, alleging that the company had failed to live up to its "side deal" to remove the unpopular employee. The company tried to get the suit dismissed on the grounds that the contract gave it the "sole, exclusive, and unreviewable right to select its employees." In the old days this type of case would have been thrown out of court so quickly that it probably would never have been filed in the first place. However, in this particular case, the court, in a one-line opinion, let the case go forward. The other side successfully argued that having the sole and exclusive right to "select" employees

119

did not necessarily mean having the sole and exclusive right to "keep" its employees on the job.

Pleeease! The right to "select" someone is meaningless if the other side can immediately elect not to "keep" him. There is no ambiguity here, yet what seemed like a clearly prohibited side deal became the driving force behind a costly lawsuit. The moral of that story was quite apparent: companies can't depend on their contracts to protect them from side deals made by their employees. In such circumstances, someone will contrive a contractual ambiguity that will put a side deal before the jury.

## WHERE THERE'S A WILL THERE'S A WAIVER

For several years it seemed that parties that wanted out of their contracts used ambiguity as their principal tactic. In my experience, ambiguity is now the second-most likely way your opposition will get out of the deal. A *waiver* is now the preferred means because it is so easy. The waiver argument is always the same. If the other side does not like a contract requirement, they just say that at some time during performance of the contract, someone at your company did not enforce the provision in question. In other words, there was a side deal that a term would not be enforced.

Here is an example. You hire a company to build your new office building. The schedule says that the foundation has to be laid by March 1, the structural steel has to be in by June 1, and the building has to be ready for occupancy on August 1. The contract states that no changes may be made to its terms unless you issue a written modification. March 1 comes around and the company has not quite finished the foundation. They say they will be only two days late on the foundation. Your site inspector says the following three words: "no big deal." The foundation is then completely installed *two days* later.

However, assume that due to the gross incompetence of the contractor's structural team, the building is not ready for occupancy until December 20, over *four months* late. Your company has had to go through the nightmare of temporary quarters and has lost $100,000 from this four-month schedule slip. You sue. You allege that the contractor breached its August 1 completion commitment. The other side's response is as predictable as a bad sitcom. The contractor files a statement in court that says, "As early as March 1, the company inspector expressly and explicitly waived the schedule, rendering all subsequent dates void and unenforceable." What this means is that by saying "no big deal" to a two-day delay on the foundation, your company made a side deal that meant that none of the schedule commitments had to be met.

This of course is a bunch of well-cut baloney. You probably will win the lawsuit. But it might cost you $50,000 to do so, and American courts almost never award attorneys' fees in this kind of a case, so you end up a loser even if you win. Again the lesson is clear: if you are not prepared to enforce the contract as written every time, you can give up on trying to enforce it any time before the jury hears about it.

## INTERFERENCE AND TOTAL COST CLAIMS

If a company has spent a lot more than the contract price carrying out the job you hired it to do, it is going to try to figure out a way to get the money it lost back from you. The other company's goal is not to admit that any of the overrun is its own fault. It can try to get you to pay by relying on "ambiguity" or "waiver" arguments.

The problem with such arguments in the context of pervasive performance problems is that the party trying to get out of the contract has to come up with a different ambiguity or act of waiver for each contract term that it wants to avoid. This process is too inconvenient for most companies, and they usually cannot come up with enough examples of ambiguity and waiver to cover nearly all of their overruns. Consequently, when a company wants to get back a huge overrun covering all aspects of the contract performance, it is likely to make an "interference" claim. They allege that your company had so many people saying so many different things that the whole contract is void and has just become a cost-plus-profit effort. In other words, they get all of their costs plus profit regardless of the contract price or terms. All the time and money your people spent to help the other side get through its problems, often at their request, is suddenly represented by the lawyers as a confusing, inconsistent set of "side deals" that sent the poor overrunning company into a tailspin. Often the party alleging interference does not even have any specific quotes from your employees. They just testify that there was "micromanagement" or "confusing multiple points of contact" that caused increased costs. Again, they might not win the case, but they will put you through hell first, and they might force you into a settlement.

Your people should know that any informal advice or guidance that they give to a floundering supplier or customer will be twisted into "interference" by the trial lawyers. If you do help the other company, you must do it through formal contract processes and contractually authorized means. No side deals.

## IMPLIED SIDE DEALS

We have covered the "ambiguity" claim, which allows introduction of specific *precontract* statements that run contrary to the contract. Next we discussed the "waiver" claim, which allows the introduction of specific statements made *during performance* even if they run contrary to the contract, and the "interference" claim, which lawyers present to the jury without even citing specific statements. Now let's talk about "implied contract" claims, which, believe it or not, are put to a jury when both sides acknowledge that *nothing* was said by anybody!

Courts seem increasingly likely to let a jury "infer" a side deal by virtue of the circumstances alone. Let's go back to the case of building an office building. Your contract states that the builder will use aluminum wiring but it only has copper wires, which are a lot more expensive. The construction company installs the copper wires, and your inspector says nothing. The builder does not even tell you that the copper wires will cost $30,000 more than the aluminum wires until it sends the bill. You refuse to pay for anything over the cost of the aluminum wires specified in the contract. The builder sues on the grounds that there was an "implied" side deal. Your guy saw the copper wires and said nothing so he implicitly agreed to it.

This isn't that far-fetched. Cases like this are filed and go to juries all the time. In a very well-known example, a large company spent around $290 million over the contract price on enhancements to a huge development project and argued that most of them had been "implicitly" approved by the customer. The company won a $200 million settlement. And it won without ever citing a specific act of approval by the customer.

So not only do you have to stick to the contract as written, you have to avoid acquiescence to extracontractual efforts of a third party that might be looking to you to foot the bill. Seeing something contrary to the contract and not speaking up or simply accepting the benefit of another company's unauthorized labor can easily rope you into a lawsuit and might even result in serious liability.

## HOLES IN THE PAPER

Lawyers and the court system have made it tough for business people to perform their contracts without every little side conversation getting in the way, but business people have plenty to be ashamed of as well. At least a third of the cases involving "side deals" that I have handled were not brought about by a creative lawyer. No one needed to allege ambiguity, waiver, interference, or implied deals to get beyond the contract. Rather, in these cases, the contract was so badly worded at the outset that it asked for—maybe even *required*—a side deal in order to be effectuated. Here are some examples.

## TBDs

TBD stands for "to be determined." It should stand for "totally blows the deal." Often in the excitement to get a deal done, whether it be a hardware or software design, a new product, or a service, parties sign contracts stating specific prices and schedules but not fully defining the product or service to be purchased. I have seen contracts literally littered with the letters "TBD" in key areas.

For example, a contract says that a company is going to get $25,000 to develop within four months a computer program that writes a love poem if the user puts in the name of the recipient and some of his or her favorite things. Then there are lines in the contract that use TBD to define the average length of poem, the number of "favorite things" that can be included, and whether the poem can rhyme at the user's option. These TBDs mean that there *has to be a side deal* for the program to be written. There are essential terms missing that must be defined for the project to go forward. Certainly, if the customer decides that the poems have to be at least 5,000 words in length, incorporate at least 100 nouns, and rhyme in the manner of a Shakespearean sonnet, the writer of the program is going to want more than $25,000 and probably more than four months to do it. Most courts would sympathize with the software developer in this case. When you have terms that are that wide open, you really have no contract at all.

The problem with TBDs is not limited to esoteric software contracts. I have seen or heard of multiple TBDs rearing their ugly heads in major defense contracts, catering contracts, agency and sponsorship contracts, in a loan agreement (where the interest rate was TBD!), and even in a couple of trusts. These agreements are often worthless and can result in major litigation as the parties bicker over the side deals that supposedly fleshed out the TBDs.

## Vague Standards

In the heady zeal to set out toward a new and exciting goal, often parties sign agreements that state the goal but that do not define who has to do what to achieve that goal. This is particularly true in marketing and public relations agreements and joint ventures. A couple of years ago, one of my clients became a celebrity of sorts in his field. I got caught in a real mess when I did not successfully talk him out of signing a contract in which he paid a lot of money for a self-proclaimed marketing guru to use his "best efforts" to promote my client in his industry.

The goal of "promotion in the industry" was defined, but what had to be done to achieve that goal was stated only as the "best efforts" by the marketer. My client thought "best efforts" meant that the marketing person would serve as an advance man at all public appearances, write articles, line up interviews, and the like. The marketing guy thought his job was to clip articles and make an occasional phone call to a local media station alerting it to the arrival of my client. Many heated discussions ensued. Both sides screamed and yelled about all the promises, i.e., side deals, they had made about attending or not attending events, writing or not writing articles, lining up or not lining up interviews. It went on and on. A contentious arbitration followed that ended up draining both sides financially and emotionally, only to end in a settlement stalemate.

> Phrases such as "best efforts," "reasonable efforts," "every effort," "in accordance with normal practice," "as is reasonably necessary"—you catch the drift—are almost as dependent on side deals as TBDs are. They leave key requirements to the often inconsistent opinions and memories of the parties and cause a lot of unnecessary lawsuits. Avoid them or be prepared to spend a lot of time and money arguing that the other side is lying about a side deal that allegedly gave meaning to the vague standards you put in your agreement.

### CONFLICTING TERMS

Another way business people open themselves up to arguing about side deals is to have an agreement with patently conflicting terms. For large companies, this situation most often comes up in transactions that involve long standardized contracts that are incompletely tailored to a particular transaction. For example, sales of assets, mergers, consignment contracts, corporate acquisitions, bond issues, major real estate sales, major construction contracts, and major government subcontracts are usually governed by "general" terms and conditions that tend to apply to all such transactions. These terms, which can go on for hundreds of pages, are then either tailored to an individual transaction or supplemented with "special terms" that reflect the unique circumstances of the particular deal at hand.

Frequently after the tailoring is complete, no one from either side goes through the whole document to make sure that all the special terms are consistent with the general terms. The result is two contract provisions, often a hundred pages apart, that are totally irreconcilable. For example, not long ago I saw a contract that said on page twenty of the general terms that the contract incorporated all provisions of the Uniform Commercial Code. About sixty pages later in the special terms, the contract stated that it would be governed by the Federal Acquisition Regulations. Unfortunately for the contracting parties, the Uniform Commercial Code and the Federal Acquisition Regulations differ on some key points. If a dispute arises and there is a conflict between these provisions, people on both sides will allege side deals and understandings, and off to the courthouse they go.

There is no excuse for this sort of business carelessness, yet it happens every day. After you have been negotiating in the trenches for a while, you have to take a breather, step back, and look at the whole deal to make sure it makes sense. This process will go a long way to keeping side deals on the sidelines in large, complex transactions.

Small businesses frequently run into the problem of conflicting contract terms as well but usually in a different context known in legal circles as "the battle of the forms." For example, a small company offers a product or service to a potential customer by sending it a form that describes the product and quotes a price. On the back of the form is a lot of fine print comprising the offeror's standard terms of sale. The potential customer or "offeree" responds with an order for the product or service. The back of the offeree's order form contains its own standard terms of purchase.

Often the offeree's fine print contains terms that are either not included in the offeror's standard terms, or, worse yet, that are in direct conflict with the offeror's terms on important issues such as payment, penalties, termination rights, and which state's law will govern the contracts. Under old common law rules, the last form sent by either party governed their relationship, so in the past, the customer usually got its way, and there was little room for misunderstanding.

However, in an effort to be more equitable, states have adopted commercial codes that alter this rule in cases involving the sale of products or goods (as opposed to services, where common law still governs). Unfortunately, the code language adopted by most states to deal with the battle of the forms is, to quote a colorful Kansas judge, "a murky bit of prose," which often leads to lawsuits alleging side deals that purportedly express the true intentions of the parties.

Under most commercial codes, the only way that you as either the buyer or seller can avoid confusion in the battle of the forms is through a written "notification of objection" to any terms that you do not like in the other side's form, followed by a written concurrence between the parties on the governing terms. That means you have to read and understand the fine print on your own forms—something few employees do—as well as the fine print on the other side's forms—something even fewer employees do. Then you must compare the two forms by noting both additional terms and conflicting terms and notify the other side of any terms to which you object. Finally, you have to reach an agreement on which terms will apply to the transaction. Only then can you conquer side deals in the battle of the forms. I cannot tell you how many thousands of lawsuits would have been avoided had this simple process been followed.

Spending a couple of hours reading fine print is not fun for anyone, but it is not as bad as spending a couple of years of writing checks to your attorneys. An often unexpected benefit of this exercise is that you will learn more fully the protections contained in your own contracts and you may get some ideas for your contracts by reading those of the other side. On a number of occasions, I have been called in to a dispute late in the game and seen correspondence in which one or both parties stated their positions—usually relying on side deals—without even citing the key contract provisions that supported them. Typically, I then learn that the parties in question did not realize that they had such a contract provision to support them because no one involved ever bothered to read the contract!

# MISTAKE NUMBER 8: MISUSING YOUR POWER

You've heard the cliché that with power comes responsibility. But the truth is that with power comes liability. Power makes people feel invincible, but the more power you have, the more legal exposure you have. The law holds powerful people and their companies to a higher standard of conduct than normal people and their companies in almost every area of business. Many companies and their employees get into trouble because they do not understand the legal vulnerabilities associated with having the ability to affect and influence others.

You do not have to be making six figures to be powerful in the eyes of the law. This section is not only for the corporate CEO and the board of directors. Millions of people have power. For example, as agents for their company, all employees of large companies wield the full power and authority of their companies when they deal with smaller companies. This section is directed to every employee of IBM, General Motors, and other industry giants.

But there are also powerful people in small organizations. For example, any organization, no matter how small, that sells directly to the consumer has power. Under the law, the consumer is on the lowest rung of the power ladder, so the law defines you and your company to be in a position of power whenever you provide goods or services to consumers. Salespeople, telemarketers, retailers, restaurant owners, doctors, lawyers, and stockbrokers—all of these people have power over individuals. In addition, as we will see, in some circumstances, the law now even recognizes that one large company can have power over another large company. So don't think you have to be smoking a cigar at the country club to wield power.

The basic rule to remember about how to exercise power appropriately is that the law controls power with *duty*. When you are in a position of power over something or someone, you take on additional legal duties, often without even knowing it. Wielding your power without acknowledging, understanding, or accepting your corresponding duty is a major cause of lawsuits. We will first discuss the duties associated with power over individuals and then cover the duties associated with power over other companies. Interestingly enough, over the past few years, these duties have become more and more alike. So even if you do not deal directly with individuals, the duties owed to individuals will have relevance to your dealings with other businesses, and vice versa.

## POWER OVER INDIVIDUALS

If your business deals directly with individuals, you have power over them. The following are the kinds of power you have over people: power over the product, power over services, power over the transaction, power over information, and power over the premises. I will define these terms and then discuss generally the corresponding duties that go with each one. By exercising your power consistent with the corresponding duty, you will help keep your company out of court.

### POWER OVER THE PRODUCT

If your company makes a product and sells it to the public, you have total power over the design, manufacture, packaging, and display of that product. You can hide a design defect, ignore a manufacturing flaw, fail to warn about a danger, etc. You have power over the product and the consumer is at your mercy.

A hundred years ago, a company was liable for the injuries caused by its products only if the injured party could show that the company had been *negligent* in its design or manufacture. This standard allowed companies to retain tremendous power—too much power—over the product. Consumers rarely recovered their losses or were compensated for their injuries because they had to take on the Big Company in order to do so. Few consumers hurt by a product had the resources to sue the company and get its documents or take the testimony of its employees. They didn't have enough information to determine the act of negligence that had caused the defect in the product that resulted in injury. Under the negligence standard, companies could be careless, even unconcerned, about the safety of their products because few consumers could prove that the company was at fault.

However, the law has evolved to put an unprecedented duty on companies that provide products to the public. In part because of the difficulty of a small consumer to prove the negligence of big manufacturing companies, the courts decided that if a company designs or manufactures a defective product for the consumer or even sells such a product as part of providing a service to the consumer, the company could be held to a standard known as *strict liability*.

Strict liability is liability without proof of fault. The consumer no longer needed to prove that the company did anything wrong when it designed, manufactured, or sold the product. The rule became and remains that if someone is hurt using your company's defective product, your company pays. For example, if a child is hurt by a defective toy your company manufactured, you will pay. No one has to prove that you were negligent in your design of that toy. The damaged party simply has to show their injury and collect. Similarly, in many states, if a patron gets food poisoning from a dish that your restaurant served, you will pay. No one has to show that your ovens were unclean or that your workers did not wash their hands. He simply shows the hospital records of having had his stomach pumped, and he can go directly to the bank with company cash. The courts decided to protect the consumer by allowing him or her to recover based on evidence that he or she had used the product and suffered an injury.

This standard eliminated the "burden of proof" that had been the basis of American jurisprudence to that point. We all know that criminal defendants may be convicted only if the evidence shows guilt beyond a "reasonable doubt," and civil defendants are normally liable only if the other side can show wrongdoing by "a preponderance of the evidence." These are both fairly heavy burdens of proof. Consequently, people and companies normally have acted not only on the basis of what was right or wrong but also on how likely it was that anyone could prove that they were wrong.

With strict liability, there is no longer a burden of proof. If you sell a defective product or service to the public and hurt someone, you cannot get away with it. Strict liability is the duty that comes with power over the product.

There are, nonetheless, a couple of qualifications and exceptions to the strict liability rule. The plaintiff has to show that the product was defective, but that requirement can be met with testimony as meager as "I heard something pop and the next thing I knew the car crashed." And companies can raise the defense that the consumer misused the product. Even that minor exception, however, has been whittled down by the courts so that companies can be liable for the "foreseeable misuse" of their products. The last defense that companies have is in placing "warnings" on products, but sometimes even a well-worded warning does not defeat strict liability.

The strict liability standard is a message to companies that cutting corners is a major misuse of power. Just read the newspapers and you'll see that many companies that manufacture consumer goods have employees who do not always adhere to quality or inspection requirements. Such cases are reported every week, and some are catastrophic. There is still a mentality among a limited number of corporate employees that they can get away with carelessness in their design, manufacture, or handling of products and that no consumer who buys the product a year from now or a thousand miles away from the plant will have the time or money to track down the laziness that went on in the company's processes.

Cutting corners is a dangerous situation for companies. The company always pays for the damages, but since no proof of individual negligence is required, often the guilty party remains anonymous.

The abuse of power by unreliable employees costs companies millions of dollars. The proper corporate response is to educate employees about the implications of strict liability and to create a clear company policy requiring that violations of quality, inspection, or safety standards be immediately reported to a designated individual. The policy should further state that the failure to report such a quality lapse is grounds for dismissal. That is literally the only corporate weapon against the burdensome duty known as strict liability.

## MISTAKE NUMBER 8: MISUSING YOUR POWER

### POWER OVER SERVICES

The strict liability standard has not yet permeated service companies. If you provide a product as part of a service (such as food at a restaurant or a part to repair a refrigerator), you may be responsible under a strict liability standard. However, "pure" services are not held to such a standard. If you organize a cruise, provide technical advice to NASA, or write a column for a newspaper, liability for not doing your job is dependent on the injured party proving negligence, incompetence, a breach of contract, or, in the case of the press, libel. There remains a heavy burden of proof.

The law does however recognize heightened duties in some relationships between service providers and their customers. These are called fiduciary relationships. A broker or trustee who has discretionary control over your assets has a fiduciary responsibility to you. Lawyers have similarly heightened duties to their clients. A fiduciary has the duty to put the interests of the client above personal interests at all times. The punishment for breach of a fiduciary relationship is civil damages in most cases, but under many state and federal laws, breach of fiduciary duty can result in criminal penalties as well. Employees at many banks, brokerage houses, and trust companies have gone to jail for commingling their personal interests with those of their clients.

Often fiduciaries breach their duties because they think they can act in a manner that will benefit themselves but not hurt the client. A bank executive might recommend to its depositors a risky investment because he or she honestly believes that it will make money. But if the bank loses the investors' money without having fully disclosed the risks, it has breached a fiduciary duty and possibly committed a criminal act. A trustee who invests a client's money in a real estate partnership owned even in part by the trustee has intermingled his or her own interests with those of the client and has, almost by definition, breached the fiduciary duty inherent in the relationship.

Discretionary broker-client relationships and trustee-beneficiary relationships are among the most common types of fiduciary relationships, but the law is nebulous enough to imply fiduciary relationships in less standard scenarios. If your company offers any service for which the purchaser places its trust and confidence in you, you are open to a claim for breach of a fiduciary relationship. That means that if your

133

company deals with the elderly, the ill, or the infirm—maybe even the ignorant—you will, as a practical, and often a legal, matter be held to a level of responsibility equivalent to that of a fiduciary duty. In fact, the greater the disparity between your power and the customer's weakness, the more likely you are to be held to a higher standard of duty. Remember that in today's world, taking candy from a baby might well land you in jail.

## POWER OVER THE TRANSACTION

When you are dealing with individual consumers, the old clichés of "buyer beware" and "read the fine print" have practically gone out the window. If your employees think they can force a consumer to accept your company's terms by handing them a form with lots of small print on it, guess again. There is no "battle of the forms" here as there often is between companies doing business together. Courts will frequently refuse to enforce what are called "contracts of adhesion"—contracts between a company and consumers, usually composed of a form written in small print on the back of a receipt, ticket, or invoice. Because such contracts often represent an abuse of power by companies, they are often not worth the paper they are written on.

For example, my wife once bought an auto alarm. The form on the back stated amid hundreds of tiny words that if warranty work was required, the consumer had to bring in the *original* receipt or the company would charge something like $50 for "receipt location." The alarm broke a week after the company installed it. My wife went to the store and asked the salesman to repair it. The salesman asked my wife for the receipt but she said that she could not find it. The salesman freely admitted that he had a copy of the receipt in a file cabinet right behind his desk but that he would not lift a finger to get the receipt unless my wife paid $50—half the price of the alarm!

The matter was resolved without a $50 lawsuit, but, had it gone to court, no judge would have allowed the company to get out of its warranty requirements by charging $50 to open a file drawer. Courts refuse to enforce what they call "unconscionable" provisions of consumer "contracts of adhesion." These can include provisions that require a consumer to make accelerated payments when they miss an installment, or that require a consumer to pay penalties that are out of line with the actual damages suffered by the company, or that allow the repossession of more than what the consumer initially bought. These are arrogant assertions of superior bargaining power and will simply go nowhere in court. In some states, onerous contracts of adhesion will get your company into trouble with the state's attorney general, not to mention the local consumer reporter. They are not worth it.

### POWER OVER INFORMATION

Another major kind of corporate power is over information. The information that gives you the most power is "inside" information—that which is not available to the public. With such power comes major duties. There is in fact a fiduciary relationship between the company's corporate directors, senior officers, and the stockholders of your company. The senior officials cannot put their personal motivations above stockholders' interests. For example, they generally cannot go out and buy a lot of company stock right before they release a great earnings statement, and they cannot sell a block of stock right before an announcement that the company has lost a big client.

At the beginning of this section, I noted that you do not have to be a big gun to have power and its associated duties. Not surprisingly, therefore, insider liability extends beyond the fiduciary relationship between the big guns and the shareholders. Courts have extended the duty not to profit from inside information to employees at lower levels in big companies and even to corporate outsiders who receive tips from an insider.

This is the law of insider trading. It involves more than the breach of a fiduciary responsibility. If your company is subject to federal securities laws, insider trading is a federal criminal offense. Sometimes it may seem very counterintuitive that you cannot use information you get at work for personal profit. After all, it is natural to assume that you should be able to benefit from those occasional special insights you get by working for your company. Unless the information is also available to the public at large, however, you simply cannot profit from it. If you do, both you and your company are potentially liable for fines, criminal penalties, and probably a shareholders' derivative suit—i.e., a suit by stockholders against the company alleging that company officials misused their power over information. Indeed, shareholders' derivative suits are becoming quite popular these days, and they cost a fortune to defend.

Legal liability for power over information extends beyond insider trading. As I stated earlier, getting official government information from unauthorized sources is now a criminal offense. Likewise, industrial espionage—accessing your competitor's customer database, stealing trade secrets or formulas, violating patents and copyrights, and ignoring data rights protections in contracts—also results in lawsuits. And as technology for retrieving and distributing information improves, it is getting more and more difficult for companies to protect their proprietary or copyrighted data. The result has been a flurry of big-dollar lawsuits when secret formulas for software, beer, soup, or perfume that may have been guarded for decades suddenly appear publicly, even over the Internet. The more widely that you disseminate improperly obtained information, the greater the damages your company will pay. Many good employees have cost their companies millions by taking their connections one step too far.

Today more than ever, corporate employees must be extremely careful both in guarding valuable information generated within the company and in using information that they obtain from outside sources. It is your duty to keep confidential information inside your company and to ensure that information from outside sources has been obtained lawfully.

## POWER OVER THE PREMISES

A company also has power over its facilities and property. Consequently the law implies certain duties that companies owe to those whom it "invites" on its premises. This is called "invitee" liability. Your company, for example, has the duty to maintain safe premises and to warn visitors of any dangerous situations. You would be surprised how many people still sue companies for the old-fashioned slip and fall in the hall and how much money a jury will award such victims. Do not forget basic maintenance of your facilities as you pursue your great business opportunities. Nothing will stop your dream more quickly than a lawsuit.

## MISTAKE NUMBER 8: MISUSING YOUR POWER

There are also a series of duties that are imposed by law that apply not only to invited third parties but also to employees and the public at large. A company, for example, has a duty to provide a safe working environment and a corresponding duty to provide the clothing and equipment necessary to render an otherwise hazardous situation safe. The government will close you down if there is any doubt about your commitment to employee safety.

An especially pressing task for companies nowadays involves the removal and disposal of hazardous materials on their premises, even if they were there before the company occupied the premises. The company can sue the previous owner and the federal government usually gets involved to apportion liability, but "environmental litigation," as it is called, is extraordinarily costly and has literally bankrupted otherwise successful companies. When your company decides to move into new premises, you have to do a full environmental audit to make sure that there is no asbestos, buried toxic drums, dioxin pavement, or lead paint exposed on the property. It is easy to ignore paint, insulation, or a little bubbling chemical pool in the back of the building when you are making your great plans in your new premises. Today, however, you have to keep your property clean to remain in the game.

## POWER OVER OTHER COMPANIES

For a long time, there was little similarity between the duties that a company had to individuals and those that companies had to other companies. While, as we have seen in the previous section, companies had tremendous duties to individuals, they had few duties to one another. Instead, the law firmly held that relationships between companies were governed by the terms of their agreements. The rule was that "sophisticated business entities" are capable of fending for themselves, regardless of their relative size.

As with so many of the old rules, there are now rifts in the "sophisticated business entity" doctrine. Within the last couple of decades, clever legal tactics have resulted in a number of cases in which one company has successfully sued another on the theory that it owed the company a heightened duty equivalent to that of a fiduciary relationship. Stunningly, some of the companies now suing others on allegations of fiduciary relationships are billion-dollar corporations—a far, far cry from the powerless individuals who first precipitated the concepts of strict liability and fiduciary responsibility.

While the number of intercompany suits based upon alleged fiduciary or similar relationships is relatively small at present, their popularity is growing at an alarming rate. Indeed, such actions threaten to be the number-one problem for powerful companies in the future. There will be a lot of them, and they *always* involve big money.

So having power over another company is now a big risk and can create new, almost frightening, duties. Fortunately, by avoiding a couple of very basic but common mistakes, you can usually nip these problems in the bud.

## POWER OVER COMPETITION

We will start, however, with a concept that is not new: antitrust liability. Antitrust laws are designed to support the free-market economy by discouraging overtly anticompetitive actions. Penalties for violation of these laws are severe. Companies that transgress federal antitrust laws, for example, may have to pay triple the amount of financial damage that they cause by their violations, and, if the conduct is serious enough, there can be stiff fines as well as jail time for the individuals involved.

As there are several lengthy treatises on antitrust law, this book cannot possibly tell you how to avoid such liability in any great depth. Interestingly, however, it only takes a couple of paragraphs to give you the kind of heightened awareness that you need to at least recognize when the company might have a competition problem. This is what law school professors call "issue spotting." Every company employee needs to learn and remember enough about antitrust law to be able to identify a potential problem. After that, you should turn the matter over to your lawyers.

Federal and state antitrust laws prohibit *conspiracies* between companies to harm consumers or other companies even by their refusal to deal with them; and they prohibit overt acts designed to establish control over the market for a product rather than competing fairly. Antitrust laws don't allow, for example, "price-fixing" at high prices that hurt consumers or lowball pricing by strong companies designed to drive weak competitors out of the market; they discourage boycotts of one company's products by a group of other companies; and they discourage companies that try to require customers to buy less desirable products in order to purchase more desirable products, a process known as "tying." For example, in 1997, the federal government (relying in part on internal e-mail) accused Microsoft of such product "tying" in connection with the inclusion of its Web browser with Windows 95 software that is preinstalled on most computers. Although antitrust law can be very complicated, you do not need to know much more than this to get at least some sense of when you might have an antitrust problem. Your company should, however, supplement this summary with some training.

What is amazing to many people, even to those with a deep understanding of antitrust law, is how little evidence is required to create an antitrust problem and how severe and unexpected the penalties can be. Also, people still tend to think of antitrust laws as applying only to tycoons getting together to play Monopoly. To the contrary, the key evidence of antitrust violations often comes from the files of typical company employees.

Take the example once told to me of two salesmen at two large tubing companies who got to be friends through a social club. Both salesmen had had a bad experience with a common competitor. One day one sent the other an e-mail that read something like this: "Just saw [other company] made a big 16-inch tubing sale to ABC hardware. I heard that they sold it at 43 cents a foot. Why don't we go in there a day apart and offer the same stuff at about 20 cents—you know, below cost. The hardware store will feel ripped off by [other company], and they'll be history."

That simple plan, which both salesmen executed, resulted in a major fine for each company and the firing of both salesmen. That e-mail reflected both a conspiracy to damage a third party through "predatory pricing" (pricing designed to drive another company out of the marketplace) and horizontal price fixing (the artificial setting of prices by companies that normally compete), and it came from the lower rungs of the company. Interestingly, these two salespeople never understood that they had done something wrong. They viewed their actions more as a college prank than as an antitrust violation. The reason they did not hesitate to execute this antitrust violation was that they did not understand the power that they had, so they could not possibly understand the duty that went with it.

It is a lesson for all of us. Your goal as an officer, executive, manager, or employee of a company should be to make a product or provide a service that is so good that no one will want to buy the equivalent product or service from anyone else. Winning the market, even the whole market, through superior quality is not and will never be an antitrust violation. As soon as your mind strays from your own product, however, and moves to thoughts of simply hurting the competition, the possibility looms large for misuse of power and the corresponding breach of duty, resulting in a huge lawsuit.

## THREE NEW DUTIES: THE BOATBUILDERS EXAMPLE

In the coming years, antitrust violations may be the least of your concerns when dealing with the competition. Some recent claims and lawsuits suggest that large companies that lose money under business contracts believe that they can convert contractual business relationships into the fiduciary relationships that previously existed only when powerful companies or people had control over weak individuals.

The legal theories that companies allege when they file this new kind of lawsuit vary considerably. Sometimes the plaintiff explicitly claims a breach of fiduciary duty by the defendant. In other cases, the company that's suing couches its claims in more standard legal terms such as fraud, breach of good faith, tortious interference with a business expectation, unfair competition, or business defamation. These are all well-known legal claims.

However, it is not important for business people to understand the different elements of proof for each kind of claim. These labels are for lawyers and are irrelevant to your business conduct. What is important is that you understand the startling new duties that companies are alleging through these claims.

All of these duties arise out of an alleged abuse of power. More specifically, they usually come from the alleged exploitation by one party of a relationship with a *third party*. I call these duties, not without some sarcasm, the duty to protect, the duty to share, and the duty to succeed.

Many of these new duty cases are between prime contractors and subcontractors and follow a remarkably similar pattern. However, the allegations in these cases apply equally well to a whole range of other business relationships, including agency agreements, distributorships and franchises, independent contracting agreements, and consulting agreements, to name a few. It is only a matter of time before they become common in these areas as well. In fact, while I was writing this book, a California judge instructed a jury that an architectural firm had a fiduciary duty of care in design to its customers—an instruction that sent shock waves through the architectural community.

Let's use a hypothetical prime-sub example that illustrates all three of these duties to see how clever and closely related they are. A customer, say the beautiful tiny South Pacific island of Bora Bora, announces plans to build its own coast guard fleet to stop poachers, sharks, and other threats to its tourist industry. The Bora Bora provincial government, as we shall call it, sends to all major international boat designers and manufacturers its five-year plan to procure seventeen new vessels, with a total potential contract value of as much as $200 million.

The plan states that the Bora Borans want two types of boats. The first is a small gunboat. The Bora Borans will issue a contract to the successful bidder for the development of one prototype gunboat with options to buy ten more gunboats if they like the prototype. If that works out, they will then plan to open competition up again for a second generation of bigger boats comprised of coast guard cutters. That competition will proceed as the gunboat competition did: there will be a prototype contract with an option for five more cutters. The plan is, in effect, two "development contracts"—one for a gunboat and another for a cutter, followed by "production options" for multiple units of each type of boat.

Let's discuss the competitors. Boatbuilders, Inc., really wants the Bora Bora contracts, but it knows that competition will be fierce. It must keep costs down. One way to keep its bids low is to line up subcontractors who are willing to keep their costs low. So Boatbuilders sends its marketers to visit potential subcontractors for various systems on the boats. The marketers give a pitch to each potential subcontractor about this tremendous opportunity to participate in a "large shipbuilding program that is sure to go on for years."

Boatbuilders decides that Ships 'n Radar, Inc. (S&R), would be a good choice to supply the radar system that goes on each boat. S&R is a large company that sometimes serves as a shipbuilding prime contractor itself, but it has no plans to compete for the Bora Bora prime contract at that time. Boatbuilders follows up its marketing pitch to S&R by writing to them, stating that it wants S&R to consider bidding on the radar subcontract as part of the Boatbuilder's "team." Boatbuilders tells S&R that "as partners," the two companies could enjoy a five-year relationship to build up to seventeen boats.

The radar subcontract is a major cost on the gunboat program. In view of the tremendous opportunity, S&R decides that it will bid the prototype radar at less than cost, a "buy in" so that Boatbuilders can keep its prime contract bid to the Bora Borans low. S&R knows that if Boatbuilders gets the production contract for the gunboats and the next contract for the cutters, S&R will recoup its loss on the initial development contract and make a very healthy profit. So S&R submits a bid for $2 million for the prototype, even though its estimates show that the cost will be about $4 million. Its bid for the production gunboat radars is $900,000 each, with costs estimated at only $400,000 each. So its profit will come from the production radars.

Boatbuilders wins the competition and gets the $18 million prime contract to build the prototype gunboat. However, at that time, a senior Bora Boran official confidentially tells the president of Boatbuilders that the Bora Boran government is low on cash and probably will not exercise the option for all ten gunboats. Boatbuilders and the Bora Borans agree to go forward with the program as structured, leaving the options intact, allowing the Bora Borans to decide later how many boats they can afford.

Boatbuilders issues a $2 million subcontract to S&R for the prototype radar. As proposed, the subcontract requires the development of a radar for the gunboat and contains the option for ten additional radars at $900,000 apiece—tracking the prime contract options perfectly.

As in all typical construction and development contracts, the prime contract between the Bora Borans and Boatbuilders contains "termination clauses." The prime contract says that the Bora Borans may terminate the contract "for convenience" at any time and pay Boatbuilders the costs it has incurred, limited by the contract price. It also says that the Bora Borans may terminate Boatbuilders for "default" with no financial liability if it performs poorly and fails to cure its poor performance in a timely manner after receiving written notice.

The subcontract between S&R and Boatbuilders contains exactly the same clauses. Boatbuilders may terminate S&R at any time and pay it the costs it has incurred up to the contract price, or Boatbuilders may terminate S&R for default if S&R fails to cure defective performance.

Boatbuilders runs into immediate problems constructing the gunboat hulls to the stringent requirements of the Bora Borans. The relationship between the Bora Borans and Boatbuilders becomes strained. However, S&R's progress on the radar development is excellent and impresses the Bora Borans. S&R starts to think that maybe it would like to be the prime contractor in the next competition for the big coast guard cutters. It arranges a meeting—without the knowledge of Boatbuilders—with the Bora Borans, in which S&R touts its capabilities and suggests that it be considered as a prime contractor for the next program. S&R representatives state that, due to their superior hull engineering staff, they will not have the same problems on the cutter contract that Boatbuilders is experiencing on the gunboat contract. They also tell the Bora Borans a rumor that Boatbuilders' program manager has a drinking problem that might be affecting his company's performance.

The Bora Borans say that they are very impressed but tell S&R that they have already decided that they cannot afford even to exercise all the options for the gunboats, much less proceed with the cutter competition. The Bora Borans say that they told Boatbuilders that there would be little money available for the options at the time that the gunboat contract was awarded. S&R is not happy to learn this fact in light of its $2 million "buy in" to the gunboat program.

A few weeks later, the prototype gunboat undergoes tests and fails, although the radar works well. The Bora Borans notify Boatbuilders that it has thirty days to cure the defects. Boatbuilders tries to correct the problems but does not satisfy the customer. The Bora Borans send Boatbuilders a notice of default termination and walk away from the project.

Boatbuilders accepts that the prime contract is over. It terminates all of its subcontracts for "convenience," according to their terms and conscientiously pays all of the subcontractors their costs up to their contract price. Accordingly, Boatbuilders pays S&R its $2 million contract price, but of course Boatbuilders does not pay them the additional $2 million that S&R lost as a result of its decision to "buy in" to the program.

Boatbuilders then learns from a Bora Boran official about the earlier meeting between S&R and the Bora Borans. Boatbuilders is livid, believing that S&R should not have gone around the prime contractor's back and met with the customer directly, especially to disparage Boatbuilders' engineers. S&R is equally upset. S&R is mad that Boatbuilders failed to tell it about the Bora Bora financial troubles that made a profit on the gunboat program virtually impossible and that Boatbuilders performed the prime contract so badly that S&R had no opportunity to recover even some of its $2 million in development losses on production gunboat options.

Both companies have a reason to be mad but do they have a legal claim? Let's discuss Boatbuilders' concern that its subcontractor not bad-mouth it to the customer. The subcontract between Boatbuilders and S&R was only for gunboat radars. Nothing in that subcontract prohibited S&R from meeting with the Bora Borans to discuss an upcoming competition for a different boat. There was no breach of contract.

Now let's talk about S&R's concerns. The subcontract between the parties gave S&R no guarantee that it would recover its development loss of $2 million on the production contracts. To the contrary, the production contracts were options, meaning that Boatbuilders had total discretion to exercise them or not to do so. Moreover, Boatbuilders had the right to terminate the subcontract for "convenience" so long as it paid S&R its costs up to the $2 million contract price. Clearly, Boatbuilders was within its contractual right to terminate the subcontract—for any reason—before or after the first prototype was built. Again, no breach of contract. Yet the two parties end up in a four-year legal battle. Here is why.

Boatbuilders sues S&R for the millions it allegedly lost when the gunboat contract was terminated. Since there was no breach of contract, suing S&R involves circumventing contract law and alleging breach of a fiduciary relationship. Boatbuilders claims that for many months before the first contract was awarded, it had cultivated a good relationship with the Bora Borans. Then it invited S&R to be part of its "partnership" or "team," thereby giving the other company the benefit of its relationship with the Bora Borans. S&R then exploited that relationship to go behind the back of Boatbuilders and meet with the Bora Borans to demonstrate its superior capabilities, thereby destroying the relationship between Boatbuilders and the Bora Borans. According to Boatbuilders, this constituted a breach of fiduciary relationship. Effectively, Boatbuilders stated that its subcontractor had a duty to protect the relationship between the prime and the customer and could not compete against it as long as the first contract was being performed.

This claim probably would have been thrown out of the courthouse ten years ago, but now some courts are allowing juries to decide if a "special" or fiduciary relationship was created by the unique circumstances of such a business transaction.

S&R responds in kind. It sues for breach of fiduciary duty as well and alleges that in order to be part of the "team" or the "partnership," it decided to take a loss on the prototype and recover that loss by making a profit on the radars for the ten production gunboats and the cutters. S&R claims that Boatbuilders encouraged it to be part of a "team" or "partnership" and allowed it to invest its own funds in the development contract. In doing so, they transformed the typical prime-sub relationship into a "special" or fiduciary commitment that required Boatbuilders to share all the information it had about the prime contract that might have impacted the investment decision S&R made and to take action to mitigate any loss that S&R might incur as the result of a change in plans by the customer. By failing to inform S&R that the Bora Borans might not exercise enough options to allow it to make a profit, Boatbuilders allegedly breached its fiduciary duty to S&R.

S&R goes a step further. It claims a second breach of fiduciary duty due to Boatbuilders' default of the prime contract. The case proceeds on the basis of an alleged duty of Boatbuilders to succeed in its performance of the prime contract. S&R alleges that Boatbuilders had solicited S&R to become a "partner" and "teammate" and to invest its own funds in the project (the "buy-in"). By accepting S&R's investment, Boatbuilders took on a special duty to protect S&R's financial interests. Boatbuilders' responsibility allegedly included performing its own prime contract effectively so as to permit S&R to recoup its "buy in." By failing to do so, Boatbuilders allegedly breached its fiduciary relationship with S&R and is now liable for the $2 million in out-of-pocket costs for the development contract and $5 million in lost profits for the production contract.

### Nipping the Problem in the Bud

The contracting parties now have an alleged duty to protect the relationship with the customer and to share information about the customer as well as to perform successfully other contracts with the customer. All of these duties threaten to further increase a company's legal exposure, which is already out of control. None of these duties are spelled out in the contracts between the parties; in fact, they appear to be prohibited by the contracts. In most cases in which such duties are alleged, there is a settlement so that the viability of the allegations is never tested in front of a jury. In the few cases that have gone to trial, the party alleging these new duties usually loses.

The result, however, is almost irrelevant. What is important is not whether such suits succeed but rather whether they proceed. In the old days, judges had the time to hold pretrial hearings and write lengthy "appeal proof" opinions dismissing such claims before they progressed too far. Today such claims might proceed until there is a trial or settlement. That means that you might win but it may cost you hundreds of thousands of dollars to prove that the other side was wrong.

Moreover, if lawyers for prime contractors and subcontractors are alleging these duties, there is no reason to think that lawyers will spare other businesses from analogous allegations. For example, if a hardware manufacturer commits safety violations and gets a lot of bad press, can the independent distributors of the hardware sue for lost profits because the manufacturer failed to perform its independent functions effectively? If a talent agency loses its biggest star due to mishandling the representation, can other actors represented by that agency get out of their contracts or recover damages on the grounds that their careers have been hurt because of the agency's reduced prestige? If an ad agency gets an account from an automobile dealership by stating that it has a Rolls-Royce account, does it have a duty to tell you it knows that Rolls-Royce is going to another agency next year? Once the terms of an agreement are out the window, the realm of potential liability is endless.

These problems can be nipped in the bud. They occur because they involve a questionable use of power—usually the exploitation of a superior position with respect to a customer or third party to cause financial loss to or gain concessions from the other contracting party. This practice is now as dangerous as exploiting a superior position over individual consumers and should therefore be employed with great caution.

## MISTAKE NUMBER 8: MISUSING YOUR POWER

### RECAPPING THE EIGHT BIG MISTAKES

The harsh exercise of contractual power will rarely in and of itself transform a contract into a relationship with heightened duties such as a fiduciary relationship. The real danger for your company lies in combining such conduct with the other Seven Big Mistakes. In fact, most big lawsuits in which these new duties are alleged involve most or even all of the Eight Big Mistakes. You may have noticed that the Boatbuilders example, which closely parallels actual suits pending right now, involved *every* mistake that we have discussed in this book. These mistakes combined to allow the unhappy parties to allege the transformation of a purely contractual relationship into a fiduciary one. While it often takes having made all the mistakes to go to court, it happens more and more often.

Let's look at the Boatbuilders example again. We'll begin with mistake number 1. The problem for S&R and Boatbuilders started with bad writing. Boatbuilders wrote S&R using some marketing mush about how the program was a huge opportunity that was "sure" to go on for years. This type of fluff is great ammunition for opposing lawyers. That statement alone is not a basis for liability, but it is a rocky start down the wrong road.

S&R then did some bad estimating when it decided to "buy in" to the development contract without the internal corporate commitment to absorb the loss if the contract was terminated. It is clear that S&R management expected a profit and had not adequately applied risk factors to its decision to "buy in," such as the probability of a reduced procurement by the Bora Borans or a default of the prime contract by Boatbuilders.

The situation worsened with speculation—statements made by people who were unqualified to make them. Boatbuilders personnel intended to "subcontract" to S&R, but then they said the relationship would be a "partnership" and a "team." Any lawyer can tell you that "partnerships" and "teaming arrangements" are legal relationships that are usually different from prime-sub relationships. Partners *do* have a fiduciary relationship to one another, and teammates under many teaming agreements have higher duties of disclosure and information exchange than do prime and subcontractors. So in order to induce S&R to make some investment or "buy in" to the program, a group of Boatbuilders employees who weren't lawyers started throwing around explosive legal terms in a very loose and careless manner, giving the subcontractor the means needed to circumvent its subcontract when things got bad. In fact, in each of the last two major lawsuits I have handled, one party was burned by telling the other that they were a "team" and "partners." It may sound nice and friendly, but using chummy terms with defined legal meanings is really just trying to get something for nothing, and it is loaded with risk unless the legal connotations are explicitly disclaimed.

The Boatbuilders saga also involved some bad research. If Bora Bora's government knew it lacked adequate funds to complete its program at the time it awarded the first gunboat contract, S&R did not have enough information about the financial resources of the Bora Borans. Obviously the Bora Borans did not have anything close to the $200 million they said they wanted to spend in their five-year plan. If I were going to invest $2 million to "buy in" under a contract with a South Pacific island, I would make sure that the island had the financial wherewithal to complete the program and let me get my profit.

Boatbuilders was also guilty of ignoring problems. It plodded on with a bad relationship, giving S&R the chance to sneak in and try to take the second project away. Then Boatbuilders was terminated for default—an action that occurred after its opportunity to cure the defects had failed to resolve them. Default termination is a severe action. If the problem got that bad, someone at Boatbuilders was not addressing problems effectively.

S&R got personal about Boatbuilders' program manager by calling him a drunk. This could well be a pivotal piece of evidence that would convince a jury that S&R had breached a fiduciary relationship to Boatbuilders. If S&R had just stuck to discussing its capabilities with the Bora Borans, there may have been no problem. However, a jury might well perceive S&R's comments about the Boatbuilders' program manager as below the belt and could use such misconduct as an excuse to find that there was a "special relationship" that precluded side meetings between the subcontractor and the customer outside the presence of the prime.

Finally, the plaintiff in each of these scenarios had only one way to bring the concept of "teammates" and "partners" into the picture. It had to come in as a side deal. Both parties would have to admit that the only written agreement between them was a subcontract. That subcontract said nothing about the duty of the subcontractor to protect the prime's relationship with the customer; it said nothing about the duty of the prime to share information obtained from the customer with the subcontractor. It also said nothing about the duty of the prime to perform well enough to protect the financial interests of the subcontractor. So whichever party is alleging these duties must plead that there was an understanding that as "teammates" and "partners," the two companies would look out for each other in a way that transcended the terms of their written contract. Each party must allege a side deal that was different from the main deal. With all those mistakes behind them, the arguably arrogant use of power by both sides took on more significance and resulted in a costly and draining legal battle that never should have occurred.

As you can see, it is easy to make any one of the Eight Big Mistakes. Companies often make all eight in one transaction. As the mistakes are compounded, the liability increases exponentially. The more mistakes you make, the more likely you are to transform hard-won deals and arrangements into costly legal battles.

The solution is easier than you might think. You do not need to look tentatively over your shoulder every time you enter a business transaction. You do not need to memorize the examples and analyses presented in the previous pages. You do not even have to memorize the Eight Big Mistakes by title. All you need to avoid the mistakes that get your company in court is context—the basic exposure to the mistakes that you have already obtained from reading this book—and commitment—an overriding determination to continually assess the potential consequences of your actions.

I call this combination of context and commitment *business precision*. You work hard to get a transaction consummated in a manner that will meet your expectations. You seek precision. Mistakes such as bad writing, speculating, and side deals all have the same effect. They make the transaction less precise. Getting personal blurs the words on the pages. Bad research cracks the foundations of the transaction. Ignoring problems, bad estimating, and the misuse of power ultimately lead a desperate party to shred the agreement to pieces. All of these mistakes undermine the business precision that you worked so hard to get.

If you keep what you have read in the back of your mind, and if you keep the integrity of the transaction in the forefront of your mind, you will not have to think about making the Eight Big Mistakes any more than you think about how to avoid wrecking your car when you drive to work. You will act with a natural business precision that will keep your company out of court. The ability to avoid the mistakes that cause lawsuits will become part of your professional identity.

# PART THREE
# The Four Shields

Remember that home improvement project we discussed at the beginning of the book? We discussed how avoiding lawsuits is not much different from remodeling your home. If we were to pursue that analogy, we could say at this point that we have finished making the structural changes. Now we are ready for surface protection—grout, varnish, tuck-pointing, and a couple of coats of heavy-duty paint, and we should have the protection that we need.

The analogy is a good one, but not perfect. The whole home improvement concept is methodical and tangible, kind of like our legal system used to be. If you want to visualize a more contemporaneous analogy for business lawsuits, you should picture your company as a fortress under attack from a technologically advanced alien craft armed with strange and untried fiduciary theories, advancing toward you with video depositions, bar-coded trial exhibits, viewgraphs, computer re-creations, technical experts, and forensic evidence.

You are going to need more than paint and varnish to protect yourself from these guys. You need high-tech shields, the equivalent of those invisible force fields in science fiction movies. Your defense has to be impressive and seemingly invincible and must address all of the other side's principal tactics.

A company that attacks you with high-tech litigation wants to hurt you in four ways. First, the company that sues you wants to break open your organization and show it to the public in the most unfavorable light possible. Your opponent wants the world to see a slanted version of what you have done. It wants your communications and internal documents taken out of context and thrust into the public domain through briefs, motions, depositions, and trial exhibits.

Second, your opponent wants to destroy the particular transaction at issue. It wants out of the deal. It wants to destroy the paper on which the deal is written.

Third, your opponent wants to bog you down in the web of our legal system. Subpoenas, hearings, depositions, document searches, trial settings, and delays all leave many companies feeling helpless and reactive.

Finally, at the broadest level, your opponent wants to disrupt your ability to conduct business in the way in which you choose. By alleging distorted relationships, breaches, waivers, ambiguity, and extracontractual understandings, your opponent wants to interfere with your capability to make business decisions with any certainty.

Consequently, if you seek truly powerful protection against being sued, you have to be able to thwart all four of these goals. You must protect the sanctity of your internal company documents and communications; maintain the integrity of the transaction at issue; avoid the pitfalls of our legal system; and reclaim control over your business operations.

You need the Four Shields. To visualize how the shields or force fields protect your company, picture four concentric circles surrounding your office building. Each circle represents one of the Four Shields that we will discuss. The circle closest to the company is the field that prevents your internal oral and written communications from causing lawsuits. The next circle from the center prevents individual business agreements and transactions with third parties from resulting in litigation. The third circle protects you from the dangers of the legal system that have developed over the past couple of decades. The final circle, furthest from the company, maintains your freedom of choice in business. It gives you the ability to make a clean break from an undesirable business situation and reclaim control over your company as a whole.

Each of these shields gets its strength by operating in areas in which the law over the past few years has become more favorable for companies that value business precision. You will recall that a common theme in the Eight Big Mistakes is that each plays into the erosion of certain long-standing legal principles that once protected the integrity of freely negotiated and consummated business relationships. It seems logical that if we are going to look to the law for protection against such erosion, we need to focus upon the areas in which the law has gotten *stronger* with respect to the integrity of business transactions. There are such areas, and they are what give us the power to develop the Four Shields that will protect your company from lawsuits.

Let's start with the shield that protects your internal company communications and documents.

# SHIELD NUMBER 1:
# THE SHIELD OF PRIVILEGE

A rubber stamp and an ink pad are very powerful tools. Every senior executive should have them. Every manager at every level should have them. Everyone else in the department should know where they are. The stamp should have three—and only three—simple words: PRIVILEGED LEGAL COMMUNICATION. Properly used, that stamp represents the shield of privilege. It will protect your documents and communications from being used against you in court, and give your company a reputation as an unassailable fortress.

Most people know about the attorney-client privilege; few know its power and even fewer fully utilize it. Defined by its traditional meaning, it protects confidential communications to an attorney, made for the purpose of securing legal advice, from disclosure to third parties. A related but more limited privilege is that of "work product," which protects materials that are prepared in anticipation of a lawsuit from disclosure to third parties.

These privileges sound expensive and of limited use. It appears that you have to hire a pricey lawyer to get them, and you only need them when you're already in so much trouble that you need a pricey lawyer. Some protection.

In addition, for a long time the law did not value these privileges too highly. Court opinions described the attorney-client privilege as "fragile" and easily waived. For a while it was unclear if a lawyer who was also an employee of your company could claim the privilege. It was also unclear if the communications between two nonlawyers acting at the direction of a lawyer to gather information or interview a witness or the like could be covered by the privilege. There were even cases that said that any inadvertent disclosure of a privileged communication to a third party waived the privilege for that and all related communications. In short, in the old days, you could not count on the privilege to give you much protection.

Things have changed for the better, and if companies want the reputation as unbeatable in court, they *must* take advantage of these developments. When you obtain the protection of the attorney-client privilege for documents and communications, the other side *never* gets to see those documents and *never* gets to learn the content of those communications unless your company wants them to. I would estimate that approximately half of the damaging documents and statements that I get from the other side in court cases could have been protected from disclosure had the opposing company made proper use of its attorney-client privilege. Companies don't use it effectively because of some misconceptions that we are going to end right now.

## MISCONCEPTIONS ABOUT THE ATTORNEY-CLIENT PRIVILEGE

### THE PRIVILEGE IS EXPENSIVE

The attorney-client privilege is actually the best deal around. If you work for a big company, you already have lawyers on staff. They are going to get paid whether you use them or not. The law now covers legal communications made between business people and in-house lawyers with attorney-client privilege. The protection is absolute and can only be waived by someone who acts with the authority of the company. It is a strong shield that costs you nothing.

If you work for a medium-sized company that has not gotten to the point where it has hired full-time counsel, chances are that one of your employees has a law degree and is licensed to practice. You can use that person to activate the privilege whenever that person is called upon to provide legal rather than business advice. Again, you can use the privilege at no extra charge.

Even small companies that have no available lawyer on staff can realize tremendous financial benefits with the careful and selective use of an outside lawyer in combination with nonlawyer company employees. It is now established in most jurisdictions that the activities of nonlawyers, including their conversations, memos, interviews, draft agreements, and notebooks are protected from disclosure to outsiders by the attorney-client privilege if these activities are part of an effort authorized by a lawyer and for the purpose of the company securing legal advice. When a potentially thorny legal issue comes up in your small company, your job is to use the outside lawyer for a short period of time and to require him or her to set up a process by which most of the work is done by your own personnel and reported back to the lawyer.

Each of these employees must, of course, be armed with the PRIVI-LEGED LEGAL COMMUNICATION stamp that goes on everything they generate as part of his or her lawyer-authorized activities. That way, down the road, everyone will know that his or her efforts were part of a privileged effort, even though he or she is not a lawyer. I know of defunct companies that would still be in business now if they had spent a few hundred dollars (or maybe a few thousand in serious matters) to start a relatively inexpensive process with lawyers and nonlawyer employees working together to address a legal issue when it first surfaced. It is a small investment with a large return.

## THE PRIVILEGE ONLY HELPS YOU
## WHEN YOU ARE ALREADY IN TROUBLE

There is an overwhelming resistance in corporate America to getting lawyers involved in anything until the business people have failed to resolve the matter themselves. The belief remains in companies that after you have failed, you hold your nose and bring in lawyers as a last resort to fight serious legal battles.

Even in-house counsel are often left out of drafting and reviewing contracts, and formulating company policy. Business people may route an agreement or potentially controversial letter to the legal department or company counsel after all the damaging unprivileged drafts have been circulated and after all the damaging unprivileged internal memos have been written, and after all the damaging unprivileged meetings have occurred in which somebody voiced strong opposition to the company position. The routing slip arrives at the lawyer's desk, sometimes with the expectation of rubber-stamp approval and no further legal involvement. At that point, the lawyer might as well give it a rubber stamp because most of the damage has already been done.

> Lawyers are not just troubleshooters. They are deemed by the law as experts, and all you need to get the shield of privilege is to seek their advice to resolve a legitimate legal issue such as determining the meaning of an agreement or a proposed agreement, the best words to use to protect the company's rights, the responsibility for performance or payment, the propriety of a competitive strategy, the relationship between a company policy or action and a law or regulation, a tax question, an environmental question, a labor question, the legal risk in the design of a product, or a host of other issues. You can establish an attorney-client privilege over virtually all communications and documents related to those legal issues. The other side may challenge your claim of privilege, but courts seem more and more willing to uphold claims of privilege these days in such situations.

The only communications you cannot cover with the shield of privilege are those relating to purely business matters—i.e., what you are going to charge the other side for your product and who is going to work on a project—and communications that further criminal acts or fraud. In other words, you cannot use the shield to hide a business decision or to perpetuate a known wrong.

Another thing you cannot do is use the privilege as a sword rather than a shield. You cannot selectively disclose privileged information to third parties and still keep related information privileged. Once you say to the other side "my lawyer says I'm right because . . ." the other side is entitled to any privileged materials needed to verify the accuracy of what you are claiming. You cannot enjoy the privilege and, at the same time, act inconsistently with the confidentiality that defines the privilege.

Later we will cover further the subject of different ways you can use the privilege through affirmative privilege programs. However, the fundamental point about privilege is that lawyers are better and cheaper when they are utilized at the front end of a transaction than at the back end after everything has fallen apart.

## IF I BRING IN LAWYERS, THEY'LL TAKE OVER THE PLACE

Business people tend to avoid lawyers because they fear that lawyers will end up running the show. Surprisingly, when it comes to control, the legal profession has changed for the better over the past several years. A couple of decades back, the mystery of the legal profession to those outside it tended to allow lawyers to take over any situation in which they were involved. The lawyer was the expert in the strange world of courtrooms and subpoenas—move over business people. A lot of lawyers still operate with the attitude that clients should shut up and do what they are told, but they will not be around for much longer because clients will not put up with it anymore.

Clients have finally realized that it is their business, money, and reputation that are at stake in any dispute. As a business person, you must remember that attorneys are hired to help you and that they work for you. Most successful large companies now use inside lawyers to manage carefully the activities of their outside lawyers, and they look for both inside and outside counsel who understand that they are clients. If your company doesn't have in-house counsel, a designated employee should manage outside counsel.

Outside law firms are rapidly moving away from broad, slow-moving structures that encourage micromanagement of the client by armies of their lawyers. They are reorganizing into smaller client-focused groups that are more like small well-trained rapid-strike forces commanded by the client. You can now define carefully what you want done by outside and inside counsel. You can and must assert control.

## THE PRIVILEGE AS AN ERASER OF MISTAKES

The attorney-client privilege can also be an eraser of the Eight Big Mistakes that we discussed earlier. I must warn at the outset that you cannot make an otherwise unprivileged document or communication privileged just by giving it to a lawyer. Don't even try to use your PRIVILEGED LEGAL

COMMUNICATION stamp on a document unless it was generated directly or indirectly for a lawyer. Misusing the privilege has gotten some companies—more recently tobacco companies— into real trouble.

However, the purpose of the privilege is to encourage the free flow of ideas, to allow candid discussion of legal issues within the company *without* the risk that those discussions will be available to a hostile third party. So once the shield of privilege is put up, it does not matter as much if your employees then engage in some bad writing or speculation. None of these documents or communications will ever see the light of day. The other side can subpoena them, but you do not, as a matter of law, have to turn them over. What powerful protection.

Here is a real-life example of a document that I received from the other side in a recent case that the opposing company could easily have shielded from us with proper use of the privilege. I had a case in which a party had experienced major cost overruns in a video graphics design contract for a major computer software company. The party attributed the overruns to a defective specification provided by the software company customer. The case went to court and we requested the other side's documents.

They produced their internal financial analysis of our contract, which their finance department had generated several months before we filed the lawsuit. The purpose of the document was to assess the exposure that the software company might have for our overruns. It mostly contained tables of numbers, but in order to assess the risk of having to pay us, the financial analysts had called a meeting with the business people to discuss their possible liability to us. As a result of that meeting, the analysts recommended maintaining a $5 million reserve in earnings to pay us for claims we might assert because, to paraphrase their report, "it appears from discussions with program personnel that we provided a defective specification to the company in several areas, including the desired level of graphic clarity, and we neglected to follow the contractual procedures to limit our liability for changes to the specification that we ultimately had to make." This was liability speculation of the worst sort, and the truth was not really as bad as the opposing company accountants thought it was, but there it was on paper without a privilege to protect it.

Once we got hold of that document, it was only a matter of time before the other side wrote us a big check to settle the matter. Can you imagine their trying to deny liability in front of a jury when their own documents showed that they were keeping $5 million dollars in the bank to pay for their admittedly defective specifications and neglect of the contract?

The other side should never have allowed that document to be generated in the unprivileged world. The company realized early on that it might have a problem, which was good, but it considered the problem to be a financial one rather than a legal one, so it called in the financial analysts. Had it called in a lawyer for a couple of hours, explained the problem, and sought some much-needed advice, the lawyer could have authorized the financial analysts to investigate and quantify the problem. Then the exercise, including the accountants' overly speculative statements would have been privileged. I use clients' in-house accounting and technical expertise on a regular basis to help me develop opinions on liability. I take the position that everything they generate and everything I generate is privileged. I believe that most courts would agree with me.

Another example of a document that gets companies into trouble is the postmortem "lessons-learned" document, to which I alluded earlier. Often after a company believes it has resolved problems with a competitor, a government agency, a labor union, a subcontractor, a distributor, or even its own performance of an agreement, the people involved get together and try to come up with policies and processes that will prevent such problems from happening again. A great idea, but it almost always involves discussions of potential legal infractions, contract breaches or interpretation, and liability assessments.

Then a lawsuit arises out of the transaction. The opposing side requests or subpoenas documents or questions your witnesses during depositions, and all of the candid discussions (maybe even some viewgraphs of a dreadfully worded report) usually go right to the other side. And they get to show the jury everything that you ever did wrong in areas that are in dispute. This does not need to happen. Corporate self-evaluation usually involves questions and issues that can be protected with the shield of privilege. Structure your self-evaluations so that you can use the privilege; it could save you a lot of money!

The basic patterns of these examples have repeated themselves thousands of times in business transactions large and small and have cost companies hundreds of millions of dollars over the years. Addressing a problem early is important and admirable; fixing a problem after the fact is equally valuable to your company. But you can usually accomplish these goals with significant legal protection by using the shield of privilege.

## AFFIRMATIVE PRIVILEGE PROGRAMS

It always amazes me how much money companies spend on consultants whose services are of questionable value. During the time I was writing this book, a major newspaper exposed a company that allegedly had been charging about $100,000 a piece to Fortune 500 companies for a detailed report on how to increase company diversity. The report that each company got was filled with trendy platitudes about "empowerment" and "mentoring." Worse yet, according to the article, most of the companies got virtually identical reports, with the name of the company changed from report to report.

I've seen companies that paid consultants $10,000 a day to educate their employees on time management. After three hours of hearing the instructor babble about "prioritization" and "focused efficiency," the only concrete suggestion that came out of the meeting was that you should make a list of things you have to do, and then do those things.

I've even heard of a company that hired a "personal debt consultant" to help its employees manage their credit-card spending. The consultant told the employees that the best way to manage credit-card debt was to charge less, look for the best interest rate, and pay more than the monthly minimum.

Companies hire these no-value-added outsiders all the time. Yet when it comes to dealing with serious legal risk, many companies do not want to spend a dime on lawyers unless they are absolutely backed into a corner. Recently, I was approached by an officer of a rapidly growing new company that had gone from sales of $5 million to sales of $300 million in four years. The company was thinking about bidding on some government contracts—a very tricky process governed by a web of complex regulations. The contracts were worth about $15 million.

Our firm recommended that we come in and perform an audit during which we would look at the company's products, discuss its goals with respect to government contracts, and produce a manual that explained all of the regulatory requirements and extra costs of doing business with the government. I quoted them $30,000 for the effort.

They smiled and said thank you and that was the last I heard from them for a while. It turned out that they went ahead and bid on a big government contract. They failed to fill out the paperwork correctly, which resulted in a criminal investigation into the alleged false statements made on government forms—a federal offense that lands people in jail for up to five years. Fortunately our firm was able to get them out of it. They spent over $150,000 in legal fees and paid a $50,000 fine. Had they invested the $30,000 up front for a compliance program, there is no question in my mind that they would have avoided a problem that ultimately cost them $200,000, not to mention the tremendous anguish and the damage to their reputation that came with a criminal investigation.

This brings us to the opportunity to discuss the systematic use of counsel. Our discussion of the attorney-client privilege thus far has been limited to spot treatment of isolated problems through the use of the privilege; just doing what we have already discussed will limit your liability substantially at minimal cost, giving your company the reputation for legal toughness that you need to help you stay out of court. To get an all-encompassing shield of privilege, however, you should probably do more.

You should consider setting up affirmative privilege programs, as I call them. As you shall see, these programs are very cost-effective. They are relatively inexpensive to implement, and they almost always result in long-term cost savings. If properly implemented, they often *make* money for the company in the short term by allowing the company to reduce reserves and book earnings.

### Compliance Programs

Most large companies (at least those that have been through a federal criminal investigation) have compliance programs, although their implementation could in some cases use improvement. We shall address that shortly.

It is, however, the fast-growing, medium-sized companies—such as the one discussed in the example above—that still need convincing when it comes to compliance programs. Typically, these are high-tech companies formed in the last ten years by a small group of technical wizards and financial visionaries. While such companies have expanded impressively, their growth has been like that of weeds—without much control or discipline. The founders, now millionaires, are dizzy with success.

This is the point of vulnerability. Every industry has its legal pitfalls. In the high-tech industry, they are often in the area of intellectual property rights. For government contractors, there is a whole set of regulations that must be added to existing industry standards. If your company produces hazardous materials as part of its manufacturing process, you've got a regulatory headache on your hands. If you import or export your product or components of your product, you must add yet another layer of regulation to your business. As you know, many of the rules of intellectual property law, government contracts law, environmental law, and import/export law are quite counterintuitive. You can incur liability and not know it until it is far too late to resolve the matter cheaply.

Some companies "wing it" and just hope that they do not mess up. Then they sound the alarm only when they realize that they have a problem. Other companies get piecemeal advice from counsel as issues come up. These approaches are neither the most cost-effective nor the safest way to ensure consistent adherence to legal and regulatory requirements. Executives at such companies need to start planning for the more orderly growth of their maturing companies. Part of that process should include the development and implementation of a compliance program.

For such companies, a compliance program involves spending generally anywhere from about $15,000 to $75,000 to have outside counsel come in and, usually in a privileged legal context, interview top executives to learn about the company's products, the market, the competition, and the intentions of management with respect to such products. Lawyers should also review existing company contracts with customers, suppliers, and joint venturers and draft an easily comprehensible compliance manual that outlines the legal and regulatory requirements governing the company's planned activities. They should provide an appendix of form contracts, regulatory requirements checklists, and applicable government forms that can be easily tailored for future company transactions. These documents will normally be unprivileged. Lastly, the lawyers should spend a couple of days educating a company-appointed executive who will serve as the corporate compliance officer, and who will be responsible for educating and monitoring other company employees to ensure compliance with the law and company procedures.

These programs work. They put much-needed discipline into fast-growing enterprises, and they save the companies a lot of money in the long term. The only problem with compliance programs, and this surfaces in larger companies more often than in medium-sized or small ones, is that companies sometimes undertake the effort to develop compliance programs but do not go the extra yard to ensure that all of their employees are familiar with them. The compliance officer, especially in a large company, needs to be given both the duty and the authority to implement the program through wide distribution of the compliance materials. In addition, he should hold regular (albeit brief) education sessions that ensure that all employees—including senior executives—are fully up to date on the legal issues that may affect their transactions.

Before you hire a stress-reduction expert to tell your workers to spend at least one minute per hour thinking of something pleasant like flowers, get your legal house in order with a compliance program. You'll be able to think of something even more pleasant such as not having to take the witness stand.

## THE 1-PERCENT RISK AUDIT

In my experience, all-out corporate litigation usually involves legal costs and fees that add up for each side to between 10 and 15 percent of the "swing"—the total amount of actual damages in controversy in the case. If I have a claim against your company for $3 million and you have a counterclaim against me for $2 million, the swing is $5 million because there is a $5 million difference between what I could get and what you could get out of the case. That means you can expect to spend $500,000 to $750,000 to resolve that matter through litigation. The $500,000 represents the cost of a business case that goes through the route of filing, responding to the other side's subpoenas and motions, hearings, a major document production, answering written interrogatories, a lot of depositions, and then a settlement. The $750,000 price tag is for the relatively rare case that has all the elements I just described, and also has to be prepared for trial and tried before a jury. None of these estimates includes the cost of the extensive internal company resources that have to be diverted to the litigation process, and remember that the general rule in American courts is you will bear your own legal costs even if you win. This is also almost always the case if you settle, because the other side will never agree to pay your costs as part of the deal.

The 1-percent risk audit replaces litigation fees amounting to 10 to 15 percent of the swing (plus in-house costs) with fees that total about 1 percent of the swing. To accomplish these savings, companies need to perform a legal-risk and -strategy analysis at the time that the problem arises rather than at the time a lawsuit is filed. It is time to do a risk audit when technical, schedule, or financial problems involving your company, your customer, your supplier, or your joint venturer endanger the transaction as a whole and/or have cost one party so much money that it will have to seek redress. Usually a company knows of such problems many months (and sometimes a year or two) before the matter evolves into a dispute that is headed for the courthouse.

The audit may be performed by in-house lawyers or by outside lawyers under the direction of in-house lawyers or an appointed executive. The advantage of in-house lawyers is savings; the advantage of outside lawyers is they bring broad litigation experience to the table and, subject to ethical limitations, can give you opinions on which you can base your financial reporting. If you do use outside lawyers, the normal rule of thumb is that they should provide you with an audit budget that does not exceed 1 percent of the swing for cases in which the swing is over a million dollars; they'll probably need 2 percent or so for smaller cases.

For that modest fee, the audit should accomplish several tasks: the lawyers should review the relevant documentation, including contractual documentation (purchase orders, franchise agreements, licensing agreements, etc.) and correspondence and interview the relevant personnel to identify the strength of company witnesses with regard to demeanor, credibility, personal hostilities, and the like. They should also assess the party likely to be legally responsible for each problem and any defenses that they might have. They should also roughly quantify the damages suffered by an injured party for each discrete issue.

Finally, they should produce a strategy for reducing the company's exposure in the transaction. The results of these tasks should be contained in a privileged memo to the company. Subject to certain American Bar Association (ABA) guidelines, outside lawyers can also give opinion letters upon which the company can base certain decisions regarding reserves, write-offs, and other matters.

These risk assessments can pay off in three ways. First, they often result in the saving of earnings in the short term. Companies that know they have a legal problem are often required to maintain a cash reserve for its resolution or to write off monies that they will be unlikely to recover. Often the sums reserved are too high because the company has not devoted adequate resources to assess the extent of the problem and then executed a strategy to reduce the associated liability. The legal risk assessment often allows the company to determine that a smaller reserve or a lower write-off is acceptable.

Just recently, I performed a risk audit for a company that had a $980,000 reserve to pay a subcontractor that it knew would assert a claim at some point. The reserve was $980,000 because its engineers thought that the company had provided a bad specification to the subcontractor. This turned out to be only partially right. The company had several legal defenses that were not within the realm of the engineers' training. As a result, I gave them an opinion that the liability was probably not as great as originally estimated. The company then designated $780,000 as earnings the next quarter and the matter ultimately settled for under $200,000.

The second way that risk assessments often pay off is that they provide a strategy to avoid litigation early in the development of the problem. In the case described above, for example, there were about four open "change orders"—unpriced contract modifications—for minor issues that had to be negotiated at the time the big problems surfaced. This opened up a possible strategy for risk reduction. I recommended that these minor matters be negotiated by well-advised, mid- or low-level employees in a very low-key way, so as not to tip off the other side to our serious level of concern about the situation. I suggested the final contract modification documents contain broad release language that would preclude later claims for a lot of money. The company followed this strategy and greatly strengthened its negotiating position when the big issues became more heated.

The last way that risk assessments can save money is that, if the case ultimately does go to court, all of the legwork has already been done and your company will be ready for the lawsuit. The factual development of a case is difficult and inefficient after a lawsuit has been filed and your company is reacting to the papers and pleadings of the other side. The same risk-assessment tasks that cost you only 1 percent of the swing early on will cost you much more once the company is caught in the turmoil of a lawsuit. Therefore, even in those circumstances in which risk analysis does not accomplish the goal of keeping you out of court, it will still more than pay for itself. And keep in mind that if you avoid only one lawsuit for every ten risk assessments, you will still come out ahead financially.

Risk assessments are another worthwhile privileged endeavor that some companies, large and small, still resist. Times are changing, however. So many companies have been stung by big litigation costs that they are now regularly requesting predispute legal risk assessments. Some businesses, such as those that manufacture products subject to strict liability do not even wait until a problem arises to perform such assessments. They do them before their product is even introduced into the marketplace. Other companies have such audits performed just before a major transaction is consummated. Hopefully, companies will continue to use lawyers to anticipate and resolve problems constructively, rather than to carry out the devastating litigation tactics that have dominated the past decade or two of American legal history.

## THE INTERNAL CORPORATE INVESTIGATION

In some cases, an internal problem is so serious that the company must undertake a more formal investigation. If someone in your company alleges that employees have engaged in criminal misconduct or serious civil rights violations, ignoring the alleged problem can, as you know, result in further charges against those who chose to do so, including conspiracy, obstruction of justice, and other serious crimes independent of the underlying allegations. The best solution for learning the truth and limiting the scope of company liability is to perform a comprehensive internal investigation.

To have credibility, these investigations must be conducted by persons independent of the company, so they should in almost all circumstances be run by outside counsel. Initially, lawyers conducting the investigation should do so under a strong umbrella of legal privilege to keep the matter confidential both with respect to the outside world and even to those in the company who are not involved. The confidentiality required to maintain the privilege has the added benefit of preventing the disruption of work during the investigation.

It is particularly important to remember that in internal investigations, as in all cases, the outside counsel represents the company, not an individual employee. Lawyers must inform each witness they interview that they cannot provide any legal advice to employees and that the company, not the individual, holds the attorney-client privilege and the right to waive it. Many companies offer to pay for their employees to have their own lawyer present for an interview in connection with an internal investigation if the employee so desires. As long as the interests of the company and the employee remain the same, they may share a "joint defense privilege" that will protect the contents of their conversations. If their interests diverge, such as in a situation in which the company elects to disclose to prosecutors the criminal conduct of one of its employees, the joint defense privilege will normally be deemed waived.

The investigation usually proceeds as follows. Outside counsel will interview relevant witnesses, draft interview reports, and review documents relevant to the allegations of wrongdoing. They will then draft a report outlining their findings, drawing specific conclusions as to the likelihood that the criminal or other alleged misconduct occurred. If the report concludes that there was no infraction or that the evidence is inconclusive, the government, if it is involved, will not usually be able to use the failure of the company to take further action to charge company officials with obstruction or conspiracy. After all, the company had the matter investigated and found insufficient evidence of criminal or other unlawful activity.

If, on the other hand, the evidence points to criminal conduct or serious civil rights violations, the company can take appropriate disciplinary action such as terminating the guilty parties. It then will frequently elect to make a "voluntary disclosure" of the conduct to the relevant authorities.

Most white-collar criminal defense lawyers take the position that a company never *has* to make a voluntary disclosure unless required to do so by statute (such as some insider trading laws). On the other hand, the government has on occasion claimed that failure to disclose a known wrong constituted obstruction of justice. Whatever the legal standard may be, voluntary disclosure has both tangible and intangible benefits. Several government agencies and the federal sentencing guidelines give credit to individuals or companies that make voluntary admissions of wrongdoing. There is also the advantage of having the public hear of a serious problem from you first. Prosecutors like besieging companies and forcing them to profess guilt. If you admit an employee took a bribe and that you have fired him or her and then you waive your privilege and hand them your investigation report, your company is going to look responsible in the eyes of the public. It becomes less likely that you will suffer the threatening consequences of a criminal investigation. There are of course no guarantees, but you certainly will have taken the wind out of the prosecutorial sails.

The shield of privilege is normally the greatest protection a company has from the use of its own communications and documents against it in litigation. The most startling benefit is the corporation's discretion to waive the privilege and make a voluntary disclosure. The power of privilege is in fact perhaps most visible in the rare circumstances in which a company decides *not* to assert it and instead reaps the equally powerful benefits of humility.

# SHIELD NUMBER 2:
# THE SHIELD OF DEFINITION

The shield of privilege protects the sanctity of your company's internal communications. The next shield instead protects the transactional expectations of your company.

When your company enters into a deal with another company, it has expectations that usually relate to providing or receiving a product or service within a specified time and at a specified price. Product, schedule, and price compose the Maginot Line of business—they are like the powerful series of fortifications built before World War II by the French to protect them against attack. Like the Maginot Line, the product-schedule-price line (let's call it the PSP line) is an ominous set of defenses against those who would deprive your company of the deal it expects. You can always point to these clearly stated terms of your deal to define your expectations.

Unfortunately, as occurred with the Maginot Line, the enemy can use new and clever combat tactics to circumvent the PSP line. Just as the Germans easily swept around the Maginot Line with the blitzkrieg, your opposition can use modern litigation tactics such as tort allegations, purported fiduciary duties, waivers, and the like to circumvent the PSP line. We have already seen these tactics in action when we discussed the Eight Big Mistakes.

You need contemporary strategies that define your relationship and its value to you so that your expectations can be neither penetrated nor circumvented by the assault of trial lawyers trying to get your opponents out of the deal. The shield of definition will help you protect your transactional expectations. This shield has two parts: relationship definition and value definition.

## DEFINING RELATIONSHIPS

The PSP line defines the *transaction*. It defines what, when, and how much. Your opposition can circumvent the transaction by redefining the *relationship*. Therefore, in order to shield you against lawsuits, your agreement must define more than the transaction; it must also define the relationship.

## LABELS, FLOWERS, AND BOILERPLATE

Most business agreements today very lamely define the parties' relationship with what I call labels, flowers, and boilerplate. These archaic conventions just do not cut it. The "label" is the title of the agreement, usually written in all uppercase letters at the top of the agreement such as: SUBCONTRACT, FRANCHISE AGREEMENT, LICENSING AGREEMENT, SALES AGREEMENT, ASSET PURCHASE AGREEMENT, etc. These titles have developed somewhat standard meanings over the years, but they provide no real guidance as to what the parties expect out of the particular deal in question. Moreover, many courts have stated explicitly that they will not rely on labels or headings to determine the nature of the relationship between contracting parties, so the labels can be legally useless.

The parties then supplement the labels with flowery introductory language known as "WHEREAS" clauses. These overwrought phrases purport to state why the parties are entering into the agreement. Here is a good example I ran into recently.

## RENTAL AGREEMENT

This Rental Agreement is entered into by [Company A] and [Company Q] on this fifth day of August 1997:

WHEREAS Company A and Company Q desire to advance their mutual interests in promoting music to the public;

WHEREAS Company A wishes to provide performers for the St. Louis Rock festival and Company Q wishes to provide stage and lighting fixtures to advance such joint interests;

WHEREAS Company Q recognizes that it has the capacity to

make available to Company A the stage and lighting fixtures necessary for Company A to perform at the festival . . .

NOW, therefore, the parties agree as follows . . .

The agreement went on to state that Company A was going to rent the stage and equipment from Company Q.

The question I usually ask is whether these elaborate "whereas" clauses that literally dominate the beginning of most business contracts really do anything. The answer is no, nothing positive anyway. First of all, "whereas" clauses have no formal legal effect. Second, they are often so stiltedly worded that they actually obfuscate the nature of the relationship. For example, the relationship between Company A and Company Q defined above is one of lessor and lessee. The band is going to lease the stage and lights. Yet the first "whereas" clause makes it sound as if the two parties are forming a charity to promote music; the second clause makes it sound as if they have a joint venture; the third one makes it sound like a fiduciary relationship—that Company Q recognizes that by controlling the stage and lights, it has the power to allow or not to allow the beat to go on! As you can see, "whereas" clauses such as these generally range from benign to counterproductive.

We move to the boilerplate—tired, old contract clauses that lawyers have lifted from form contracts that used to be on carbon paper in the 1970s and transferred to mainframe Wang databases in the 1980s, then to DOS and WordPerfect, and now to Windows. The technology has changed, and, more important, the law has changed, but the wording hasn't. Most business contracts continue to use phrases such as "this is the entire agreement between the parties and it supersedes any prior negotiations," and "this agreement may only be modified in writing" to try to limit the relationship to the explicit terms of the contract. Judges' eyes can glaze over when they see these numbingly archaic phrases, and juries may ignore them. Such phrases often fail to withstand the assault of waivers, fiduciary duties, fraud, and other torts.

## Just Say It!

Every business contract—particularly subcontracts, sales agreements, licensing agreements, franchises, and distributorship agreements— must now have a section entitled "DEFINITIONS" or "RELATION-SHIP BETWEEN THE PARTIES." It must explicitly address and neutralize the various new duties that have been alleged in business cases over the last few years. This section must protect both sides against allegations of fiduciary relationships, waivers, and reliance on performance of third-party agreements, as well as alleged duties to share extraneous information and not to deal with other companies. The language will vary with different types of agreements.

However they are worded, they must make several points explicitly clear. They must stipulate that the agreement does not create a fiduciary relationship and that the relationship between either party and any third party is completely immaterial to the requirements of the agreement. They also must state that each party has all the information that it needs to enter into and perform the contract and that the parties have no agreement to pursue any other opportunities with each other beyond those contained in written, signed contractual documents. Finally, they must say that the acceptance by either side of defective performance by the other, including in quality or schedule, does not waive any legal rights that either party may have to claim damages for such defective performance.

In the context of a prime-sub relationship, the actual contract clause might read as follows:

IX. RELATIONSHIP DEFINED: The parties understand that their relationship is a good faith contractual relationship of prime contractor and subcontractor, and that this Subcontract creates no rights or duties in either party beyond those that are defined by the Sub-contract. In particular, the parties mutually understand and agree that:

(a) There is no fiduciary relationship between the parties; they are not partners or joint venturers, nor do they have any special duties to each other that are not expressly defined in this agreement;

(b) Neither party makes any representations as to its relationship with any third party, including the customer; the prime contractor does not warrant or guarantee its performance of the prime contract;

the subcontractor is in no way restricted from pursuing other business relationships with the customer;

(c)   Both parties have thoroughly evaluated the risks associated with this Subcontract, and represent that they have all information necessary to make an informed decision to enter into and perform this agreement; neither party shall at any time assert that the other had superior knowledge material to the other party's performance or decision to enter this Subcontract;

(d)   Both parties agree that the failure of a party to take action upon a breach by a party in no way limits or restricts the nonbreaching party's remedies for such breach and shall not be considered a waiver of any legal rights.

Note that all of the language is mutual. In order to be enforced equitably, the rules should apply to both parties equally. In addition, the law implies a duty of good faith in all contracts, so the contract must recognize the duty of good faith, as the contract does in the first line. This contract also makes the *nonassertion* of any new duties part of the duty of good faith.

Most important, however, the definitions clause cannot be inconsistent with the Maginot Line of product-schedule-price. Recently I represented a very progressive manufacturing company that had put a lot of these powerful relationship-defining clauses in its contracts. The contract contained a clause in which the parties stated that they had all of the information they needed to perform the contract. Good move. However, the contract also had several TBDs (to be determined) in areas of product performance. Bad move. You cannot have all the information you need if key performance criteria are undefined. The case went to court. The court tried to reconcile the two clauses by holding that the parties had all information except for the TBD information—thereby opening the door to all sorts of tort claims and rendering the relationship clauses useless. The relationship definition clauses must be consistent with the rest of the contract language.

So hit all those crazy extracontractual duties head-on and eliminate them. If you do it mutually and in a manner that is consistent with the basic transactional elements of the agreement, you will be protected by the shield of definition. Of course, you will have to live with the deal you made, good or bad. If there is a problem, however, you will most probably resolve it without a lawsuit. With well-defined terms, neither side is likely to start the litigation game that ultimately results in a settlement anyway, after incurring a lot of legal fees.


## DEFINING VALUE

A major comfort for parties that decide to breach their contracts is the inability of the other party to quantify adequately its damages. In this era of high technology, the quantification of damages has become more and more difficult. How much money have the Rolling Stones lost to pirated CDs and illegally copied cassettes? It is impossible to quantify so no one does anything. The same problem exists in company-to-company transactions in which one company does not respect another's proprietary rights. It is becoming a huge problem.

The shield of definition is of great use here too. Another wonderful definitional shield that some very well-run companies have adopted of late is what I call value definition. They do not just define their relationships explicitly; they also define the *value* of the relationships explicitly.

Value definition has its roots in an old legal device called "liquidated damages." Courts long ago allowed parties to state explicitly in their contracts the damages that would be incurred if the other party breached the contract. There were certain prerequisites to the enforceability of such clauses that are not important for our purposes, but the point of these clauses was that you did not always have to prove your damages after the fact. Your contract could state up front the damages brought about by a breach, and, when the breach occurred, the court would simply award the stipulated sum without further analysis.

The problem with liquidated damages clauses was that few companies would agree to them, and they were usually not necessary because out-of-pocket damages were not hard to prove. These were the days where commerce involved market-priced coal or defined quantities of manufactured products with a clear retail value. Damages were therefore easily calculable.

Recently, however, the concept of liquidated damages has been reborn in new ways by companies that deal in priceless information such as those that license products ranging from software to advanced technology to secret formulas. The increased value of information today, combined with the speed with which misappropriated information can be disseminated through computer networks, means huge potential financial losses resulting from the breach of agreements governing intellectual property. Pirated CDs or software multiply exponentially as the duplicates are digitally duplicated. A secret process can hit the Internet and be available to the whole world instantly. The damages that a party suffers when another party breaches a licensing agreement or any agreement to keep information confidential are often limitless.

Here is where the concept of value definition comes in very handy. Companies that have valuable information and license it for limited use to other companies put options in their licensing contracts. They give the party buying the software, secret process, or technology the option to have unlimited ownership of that item. They then price that option as the sum of the development costs of the product or process and the expected future profits from the licensing of the product.

Suppose you want to buy the rights to use a secret program that will allow your company's computer system to be a zillion times more powerful. The developer of the program offers to license it to your company confidentially for $2,000 per month on the condition that it only be used on your twenty computers. The program developer then also requires a term in the licensing agreement that gives you an option to buy all rights to the program for $2,850,000, which represents the development cost of $450,000 plus the present value of the expected net licensing revenues from the product—$2,400,000.

You are not going to mess with the terms of that contract. You are not going to stretch the meaning of its terms. If you decide to let even one of your employees install that program on a home computer, you are taking a huge risk. If that program makes its way from your employee's hard drive into cyberspace, you are going to have to foot a bill in excess of $2 million because the option price effectively values the breach. If the matter went to court, all the licensor would have to show the jury is that you bought an option to own the whole program for $2,850,000. That must be the value that is now lost as the information floats around the world free of charge. That's what the jury will award.

The value option is a great shield. It looks like it is there for the

177

buyer's benefit, and, in some circumstances it might be, but it is also a policing mechanism for the seller that forces the buyer into literal and strict adherence to the terms of the agreement. A clear and unequivocal statement of damages will temper the willingness of a party to obfuscate the relationship.

Value-definition clauses are currently in use only in a small percentage of business contracts, mostly those governing technology licensing. However, there is nothing to prevent a company from putting such options or similar clauses in other agreements as well. In an era in which information travels like wildfire and in which the consequences of breaches are much more serious than they used to be, companies should be using the concept of value definition for all kinds of relationships.

Imagine, for example, how a value-definition clause might have helped the city that contracted for the airport runway sensors that we discussed in the earlier section about ignoring problems. If the supplier of the sensors had had to deal with a contract clause that prospectively recognized the $75,000 per day in lost airport landing fees that would result from the late installation of the sensors, that company would have found a way to get those sensors in on time, rather than relying on a lame waiver argument or the like to get out of the deal.

I also recommend that value definition be *mutual* whenever possible. If one party suggests a value option or liquidated damages for a breach by the other, then the other side should be willing to include a similar clause for its own breach. If the objective is to deter lawsuits, there has to be a downside for both parties. Moreover, where the parties have equal or similar bargaining power, the most likely way to get value definition into the agreement is through such mutual obligations.

In today's fast-paced business world, the shields of definition—defining both the relationship and the value—are something that should work their way into most transactions. They are strong protection for all parties, but companies that value predictability in their business relationships will embrace them, and those companies are the only ones that you should deal with anyway.

# SHIELD NUMBER 3:
# THE SHIELD OF PROCESS

We have already put up a shield that will protect the inner workings of your company and a shield that will protect the expectations that you have in your transactions with other companies. The next shield, which you should visualize as the third concentric circle moving outward from your company, is the shield of process. It protects you from the tidal wave that is our legal system. Nearly everyone who has recently been involved in corporate litigation will tell you that once you are in it, the system sweeps you up and takes control away from you. You need protections against the legal process, which should always be the last resort for resolving disputes.

Interestingly, you do not only need protection from suits filed against you. You also need protection against your own hasty decisions to file lawsuits. Plaintiffs—not just defendants— are often surprised by how quickly they lose control of litigation. They are led to believe that a "first-strike" lawsuit against another company will put them in the driver's seat and put the other side so much on the defensive that it will capitulate early, but this rarely happens. More often than not, the defendant becomes so infuriated at having been sued that it immediately escalates the matter by orders of magnitude. Money becomes no object; ad hominem attacks overpower rational business decision making. The defendant responds to the suit with a volley of costly and disruptive actions such as multiple pretrial motions, onerous requests for documents, lengthy interrogatories, and notices of deposition reaching all the way up to your CEO. "No one told me that would happen," said many a CEO after being hit with a notice of deposition and huge legal bills soon after he or she had approved the filing of the suit.

Recall that value definition is probably more effective when mutual. I believe that the shield of process *must* be mutual. If you use the shield of process to give you a tactical advantage over the other side in litigation, which you can do, it will only encourage *you* to file suits. Rather, the shield must make litigation less attractive and more difficult for both parties. Only then can the shield counterbalance the heady irrationality that often precedes the decision to sue. It tempers both sides' appetites for lawsuits. It encourages a settlement before the lawsuit, rather than two years and $200,000 into it.

Like the shield of definition, the shield of process most often takes the form of specific clauses in contractual arrangements. The type of contract is irrelevant—it can be used in sales contracts, franchise agreements, mergers, subcontracts, and other matters. The clauses neutralize any tactical advantages that may encourage one party to sue; they set up obstacles to any party that considers a suit; and, most important, they maximize the prospects for a negotiated resolution to disputes.

## THE RACE TO THE COURTHOUSE

These days everyone has a claim. When there is a dispute, both sides threaten to sue. About half of the business suits I have filed on behalf of my clients were instigated because my client believed it was about to be sued by the other side and wanted some of the tactical advantages that normally come with filing first.

Filing before the other side has three advantages. First, you will be the plaintiff not the defendant. Statistically, juries side with plaintiffs more often than with defendants. Second, the party that files first has the choice of "forum"—where the suit will be litigated. If my company employs half the population of Huntsville, for example, I want the case to be heard by a jury in Huntsville, not in Seattle or Chicago or in any other city where my adversary may have a major presence. Third, it is a lot cheaper for me to prosecute a suit in my own backyard than to defend a suit a thousand miles away, so there clearly are advantages to filing first.

Trial lawyers call the rush to file first the "race to the courthouse." The rule normally is that the whole case is heard where the first filing occurs. If a second suit is filed on the same issues, it is consolidated with the first suit.

A large percentage of business suits would be avoided if the tactical advantages of filing first were contractually eliminated. The shield of process puts an end to these advantages through two types of contract clauses—one designed to negate the benefit of selecting the forum and the other to eliminate the opportunity to be the plaintiff.

## THE NEUTRAL FORUM-SELECTION CLAUSE

A substantial number of business contracts contain "forum-selection" clauses that say that a suit has to be filed in a particular court or jurisdiction. Typically, the party with the stronger bargaining power puts in a clause that requires suits to be filed where its business is located. For example, General Motors may have a parts supplier in Tulsa. The supply contract may contain a clause that says, "any lawsuit relating to this agreement shall be filed in the federal courts located in Detroit, Michigan." GM has a lot of power, so its suppliers will probably have no choice but to agree to sue or be sued in GM's home city of Detroit. These clauses demonstrate the power of one party over another, but they are usually enforced by the courts.

Such a clause may cause the supplier in Tulsa to think twice before suing, but it will certainly not deter GM from filing a suit. Indeed, by making litigation difficult only for one side, such clauses almost encourage aggressive behavior on the part of the company that has the forum advantage. Moreover, where parties are of equal power, neither will normally agree to a forum-selection clause, so we are back to the race to the courthouse.

A better tactic for avoiding litigation, and a rare but growing practice in business today, is the neutral forum-selection clause. It picks a forum for lawsuits that is not in either party's backyard. The contract may be between a Missouri company and one in Florida, but the forum-selection clause states that "any lawsuit relating to this agreement shall be filed in the federal courts located in New York, New York." The obvious benefit of such a clause is that it eliminates one of the principal advantages of a race to the courthouse. You can run to New York as quickly as you want, but you are not going to get the cultural and cost advantages that you would have had if you had filed in your home city, and neither is the other side. Neutral forum-selection clauses make races to the courthouse much less frequent, giving the parties time for more rational negotiations before they put themselves at the mercy of the legal system.

Why are such clauses so rare then? First, no one wants to give up a tactical advantage, so a company either gets the clause to say that suits will be filed in its home city or the clause is left out entirely. Second, for a long time there was a question as to the enforceability of neutral forum-selection clauses. Courts were reluctant to enforce a clause that required litigation in a jurisdiction that had no connection to the performance of the transaction at issue. Now it seems that these clauses are likely to be enforced if agreed upon by two sophisticated business entities and minimum jurisdictional requirements are met. Some courts, such as state and federal courts in New York, have stated that they consider themselves to be experts in the area of business disputes, and they welcome such disputes in their courts, even if the transaction has no relationship to New York.

Another advantage of the neutral forum-selection clause is that the parties can pick a jurisdiction that has had a lot of experience dealing with their type of transaction. Domestic business disputes can go to the New York courts that handle all of Wall Street's problems; international disputes can be heard at the very experienced courts of London or The Hague; high-tech disputes might be best heard in Southern California; and steel industry disputes can be litigated in Pittsburgh. It is possible that if courts are inundated with out-of-state cases, they might start declining to hear them, but this has not been the case so far.

If the companies involved in the transaction are small, they may wish to pick a neutral forum that is not too far away, but just far enough to deter litigation for both sides and to eliminate any home-court advantage for either side. You don't want the forum so far away that it is impossible to enforce your legal rights if you really have to do so.

The simple act of putting a neutral forum-selection clause into most business agreements would, I predict, prevent thousands of lawsuits from being filed every year.

## NOTICE AND TOLLING AGREEMENTS

By eliminating the home-court advantage, a neutral forum-selection clause will go a long way to preventing races to the courthouse. However, such clauses still do not counter the advantage of being the plaintiff in the lawsuit. There is no foolproof way to stop a party that wants to be the plaintiff, but there are ways to slow such a party down.

First, parties should include a "notice of disputes" clause in their contracts. This clause states something to the effect of the following:

> Notice of Disputes. Neither party shall sue the other until after it has given 15 days written notice to the other side that there exists a material dispute, specifically citing the Notice of Disputes clause, and describing the factual and legal basis of the dispute. During that 15-day period, neither party shall file suit against the other. If any suit is filed in violation of this provision, the filing party shall be deemed to have released the other party from all claims asserted in the suit, and the suit shall be subject to dismissal with prejudice by the court.

Dismissal with prejudice means that the suit can never be refiled. The clause requires clear, written notice of a dispute and contains clear penalties for breach.

This fifteen-day window stops the would-be plaintiff in its tracks. It also gives the parties a chance to negotiate a very valuable agreement to avoid litigation called a *tolling agreement*—a separate written agreement, in which the parties agree to "toll" or stop the statute of limitations from running on any claims for a specified period, usually sixty to ninety days. This then permits the parties to agree to extend the waiting period for filing a suit beyond the normally short notice period (fifteen days in our example) that is contained in the contract. Most tolling agreements indicate that statutes of limitations are "tolled" (stopped) for sixty to ninety days and that neither party will sue during that time period. These agreements remove the pressure to race to the courthouse, allowing the parties to calm down and look at the situation rationally. Most important, they permit the parties to continue negotiations without fear of being served with a suit during a meeting. Indeed, some of the more sophisticated tolling agreements I have seen also set a schedule for meetings between the parties during the period of the agreement. If the meetings are productive but not conclusive, the parties extend the period of the tolling agreement in writing. I have seen such agreements extended three or four times before a settlement ultimately occurred.

The combination of a neutral forum-selection clause, a notice of disputes clause, and a tolling agreement virtually eliminates the race to the courthouse that has put so many unwary companies into the web of our legal system. These mechanisms force parties to resolve disputes without suing.

## FEES, PLEASE

There is a surprisingly prevalent misconception in the business community that if you win a suit, thereby proving that the other side was wrong, it must pay your attorneys' fees as part of your damages. Unfortunately, as I have stated before, the normal rule in the United States is that each party bears its own costs and fees, even if the other side's claim or defense was proven unmeritorious. Courts award attorneys' fees only when federal or state law requires such an award (in some civil rights cases, for example), or when the conduct of the losing side was so egregiously unethical that further punishment is warranted. Such fee awards are rare.

There are cases in which a party's fees exceeded the award it got from a jury. There are other cases in which a party successfully defended a suit but went bankrupt from the fees associated with the defense. You can win and still lose. But there is a way to turn the vast expense of a lawsuit into a device to prevent litigation by altering the normal rule by contract. Suppose that the loser pays. Most courts will allow parties to put clauses in their agreement saying that the loser will pay the winner's attorneys' fees, so long as such clauses are freely negotiated (i.e., they are not contained in the small print on the back of a consumer contract) and the fees are in line with the going rate. Fees being what they are, companies are going to be less likely to file suits based upon nebulous allegations if they know that a loss is going to cost a lot of money in the form of the other side's attorneys' fees.

## SHIELD NUMBER 3: THE SHIELD OF PROCESS

In cases in which both parties have a claim, the clause should state that the party that recovers the greater amount of money pays the fees. To cover cases in which the party suing is not seeking money, such as those in which the suit is to make a party perform a contract or stop a party from taking certain actions, the clause should state that the party that obtains "declaratory or injunctive relief" against the other shall be entitled to its fees.

These clauses make parties think long and hard about the quality of their cases before they sue. The losing party pays a judgment, its own fees, and the other side's fees. The combined fees often total 30 percent or more of the amount in controversy.

## THE ALTERNATIVE TO
## ALTERNATIVE DISPUTE RESOLUTION

One of the great initiatives of the legal profession in the late 1980s was alternative dispute resolution, or ADR as it is called. ADR has become *the* buzzword for those trying to reduce corporate legal costs. Industry groups have signed ADR pacts; federal regulations now encourage ADR for the resolution of disputes with the government; and courts have adopted ADR programs.

The two principal types of ADR are *arbitration* and *mediation*. While these processes have worked to reduce legal costs in some cases, there is a strong undercurrent of dissatisfaction throughout the legal profession with the results of the ADR movement so far. Let's learn from the mistakes of the past few years and develop AADR—alternative alternative dispute resolution.

### ARBITRATION

Arbitration is a dispute-resolution process by which the parties present their cases to a neutral third party called the arbitrator (or sometimes a panel of arbitrators). The arbitrator, who acts outside of the judicial system in accordance with "terms of reference" agreed to by the parties, renders a decision.

Here are a few of the many varieties of arbitration. "Baseball arbitration" is all or nothing. You state how much you want, and the other side states how much it wants. The arbitrator then picks one of the two numbers and nothing in between. That is the way most baseball and some other sports salary disputes are resolved, but it is equally available to businesses of all types. It requires some tough nerves.

Standard arbitration allows the arbitrator to award either side whatever he or she deems proper after hearing the evidence. The arbitrator basically takes the place of judge and jury and has complete discretion to fashion the relief he or she considers necessary to redress any wrong.

"Binding arbitration" is where the parties agree in their terms of reference to be contractually bound by the decision of the arbitrator. Courts will almost always uphold the decision of an arbitrator when the parties have agreed that the decision would be binding. In "nonbinding arbitration" the arbitrator renders a decision but either party has the option to disregard it and go to court to have the matter heard again.

Arbitration has been successful in reducing legal fees in some areas, particularly in labor disputes and those in which the party bringing the action is an individual and the defendant is a company. Arbitration clauses are standard in contracts between securities brokers and their clients, as well as in contracts between professional athletes and their teams. Many consumer contracts require that disputes be resolved by arbitration in accordance with the rules of very reputable organizations such as the American Arbitration Association. Securities cases, sports cases, and consumer cases usually involve few documents and few witnesses. They lend themselves to streamlined, informal procedures and usually achieve a just result at minimal cost through the arbitration process.

Arbitration between companies has been less successful for several reasons. First, nonbinding arbitration is not of much use. The arbitrator issues an award, usually without much elaboration, and if you do not like it, you ignore it and go to court anyway. So you pay your lawyers once to do the arbitration and a second time to go to court.

Even binding arbitration can be very lengthy, difficult, and costly. Arbitrators are most often successful practicing lawyers or business people, so they can be as busy and as hard to reach as judges. While arbitrators might be as inaccessible as judges, they have less power than judges—which opens the door to all kinds of aggressive, expensive tactics by unscrupulous attorneys. Moreover, you have to pay the arbitrator, whereas judges come free of charge. I know of a recent hard-fought arbitration in which there was an $11 million swing, and the costs and fees at the end for one company were $1.4 million, which is about the same amount that litigation would have cost.

The biggest criticism of non-baseball arbitration is the tendency of arbitrators to "split the baby down the middle," as trial lawyers affectionately describe it. The arbitrator does not want to make hard decisions or alienate anyone so he or she tries to compromise rather than apply the law. The result is a middle-of-the-road decision—it gives neither victory nor defeat to either party. However, once the extensive legal and arbitrator's fees are added to the mix, the practice of splitting the baby leaves both sides feeling abused, much like the legal system often does.

## MEDIATION

Mediation involves an attempt by a neutral third party to help the parties reach a settlement. The mediator does not render a decision on the merits of the case; rather the mediator looks for common ground and tries to forge a compromise. Some mediators are quite good, and many disputes have been resolved through mediation at minimal cost.

Again, however, the larger and more complex the dispute, the less likely mediation is to resolve the matter. First, the process usually does not involve extensive preparation by the mediator. Consequently, he or she rarely has enough background in the technical matters in dispute to understand what sort of compromise is feasible.

Second, mediators are trained to put cash payments on the back burner and look for more creative ways to forge compromises. They tend to suggest all kinds of possible future business transactions between the parties. Such an approach might be okay when you are talking about an individual threatening to bring suit against a company, but in larger intercorporate disputes, the mediator often fails to understand the parties' business well enough to come up with feasible ideas for future transactions. The process frequently fails in such circumstances.

## New Alternatives

Of the many people with whom I discussed ADR while writing this book, only one had had consistently good results with the traditional process. He was a lawyer for a brokerage house who found that the standard arbitration clause in brokerage contracts provided an inexpensive, effective process to resolve disputes for all parties. Everyone else I interviewed, from those who had tried ADR in disputes with the government to those who used it for major intercorporate problems, expressed feelings ranging from ambivalence to hostility. The shield of process is not much help if it results in the same kind of disillusionment that the court system often causes.

So we need to look for something different. While arbitration and mediation are viable options that disputing parties should consider, there are a couple of less-known forms of ADR that are just now beginning to enjoy success. I have resolved several multimillion-dollar disputes in the past three years as a result of using these methods. These closely related processes are referred to as senior executive presentations and early neutral evaluation.

### *Senior Executive Presentations*

When a dispute appears to be headed to the courthouse, the big boss—the CEO or at least the head of the division—usually gets a briefing from the outside lawyers who will represent the company in the lawsuit. In most cases this senior executive knows only a little about the case before the briefing; if the company is big enough, he or she may have no previous knowledge of the problem. The briefings are full of glowing statements about the quality of the company's case. They tend to be long on rhetoric and short on evidence. They rarely mention the probable costs of taking the case to trial. While your lawyers are giving your CEO the briefing, the other side is giving its CEO the same kind of story.

A CEO's time would be better spent trying to resolve the matter himself or herself. The CEO, or some other very high-level official with no direct involvement in the dispute, should take the following carefully structured steps. The CEO should send a letter to his or her counterpart at the opposing company, inviting that person in for a senior executive presentation. If the invitation is accepted (which it almost always is), the two pick a time and a place to meet. They agree to include only themselves, their lead outside lawyer, and either their lead in-house lawyer or, if the company has no in-house lawyer, the lead in-house business person who is working on the problem. There are only three people per side. They invite none of the people who caused the dispute, and none of the people whose personal agenda may interfere with the process.

Prior to the meeting or right at the beginning, the senior executives sign a statement stating that neither side will use the statements made in the meeting against the other side in any filing, argument, or trial and that the meeting is subject to the "settlement privilege" that protects offers of compromise from being introduced as evidence at a trial. That way the parties can exchange information and opinions candidly.

Then each side has one *uninterrupted* hour to give a presentation, normally with viewgraphs, on why it believes it will win the case. The presentation, usually shown on an overhead projector, should be a well-organized synopsis of the case each company intends to present to a jury. It should represent your best case put forward as succinctly as possible. In effect, each side puts on a one hour mini-trial, with opening statements, evidence, and closing statements.

The opposing CEO will see all of the then-known evidence that hurts his or her company, not just the rosy things that the company's lawyers and employees would normally show the CEO. In fact, knowing that the other side will show its best evidence at the presentation, each company's lawyer gives the CEO a pre-meeting briefing with a much more evenhanded assessment of the situation. Such briefings are a good idea and should also be used to give the senior executives an idea of what kind of settlement the company might be willing to accept when the two executives meet.

The two one-hour presentations also provide the senior executives with a chance to see how well prepared its own legal team is and how well prepared the opposition is if the case goes to court. The company and its lawyers are putting themselves on the line. The senior executives should also require that each side independently determine the likely cost of taking the matter through a trial and should present those numbers as well.

When the briefings are over, the senior executives may spend a few minutes asking the presenters questions, but the parties must agree that there will be no arguments, no point-counterpoint. Then the senior executives go into a room by themselves and talk about the settlement.

These sessions between the senior officials tend to be very productive. High-level executives with no emotional attachment to the matter hear both sides of the story, assess the relative strengths of the legal teams, and get an idea of how much this battle is going to cost. These are the ideal conditions for arriving at a realistic settlement.

Moreover, because the whole show is just for them and because they are supposed to be the corporate leaders, the senior executives tend to be very conscientious throughout this process. The process leaves it up to them to get the company out of this mess. Every time I have participated in one of these presentations, the case was either settled on the spot or the meeting served to open a dialogue that ultimately resulted in a settlement. Often the two senior executives become friends or at least develop some mutual respect and start to build a new relationship. I cannot promise that result every time, but I can promise that this relatively inexpensive, simple process will maximize your chances of avoiding the courthouse. The identical process may also be used to settle lawsuits that have already been filed.

### *Early Neutral Evaluation*

What drives the senior executive presentation format is that both sides have to perform in front of a couple of very powerful people. The truth has a way of coming out in such circumstances. There may be, however, some companies whose senior people do not want to get involved in senior executive presentations. There is an alternative that achieves almost as good a result.

Early neutral evaluation (ENE) involves the parties' selection of a well-qualified neutral person to hear their case. The parties then give pretty much the same presentation to that person that they would have given to the senior executives with the same agreement not to use anything discussed at the ENE in any subsequent litigation. Because of the explicit evaluation that goes on in ENE each side may need a couple of hours for their presentations. The best person for the job of evaluator is a retired judge, an eminent trial lawyer, or someone else who has a good feel for how a judge might rule or what a jury might conclude at trial.

However, in contrast to the format of the senior executive presentation, the neutral person who hears the presentation is *not* there to broker a settlement. ENE is not a mediation, and that should be made clear to all involved—especially to the neutral evaluator. Nor is ENE an arbitration—the neutral party will not award a sum or other legal relief. Rather the evaluator will listen to the presentations, ask each side a series of questions, and take an hour or so to make some notes. Then the evaluator will give a candid, preferably blunt assessment of each side's case. If one side does not have a prayer of convincing a jury of a key point, the evaluator should say so. If one side seems disorganized and lacking a legal theory, the evaluator should say so.

After hearing the evaluator's oral briefing, the parties should return to their companies. The evaluator should type up a brief report consisting of about five to seven pages, and send it to each side. The parties should decide beforehand whether that report can be used as evidence in subsequent proceedings. Finally, the report should include a date and time for the parties to meet after they receive the report. With a candid neutral evaluation of the case in hand, the parties will be more realistic about their settlement goals, and the matter always has a better chance to settle than it did.

Some courts now have programs that encourage ENE. The problem so far has been that parties tend to prefer court-approved mediation programs over ENE because they either fear the candor of ENE or they do not understand its value. In addition, a few companies have had bad experiences with ENE because the evaluators, who often do a lot of mediating, do not understand their roles clearly. They want to be nice to both sides or suggest some settlement alternatives and the candid evaluation process that the parties expect degenerates into a lukewarm mediation.

Companies should give ENE a try. Like the senior executive presentation, this process is quick and relatively inexpensive. It can be very valuable if it is well structured and the parties clearly understand their roles. It can be the shield of process that protects you from the much less controllable legal system.

# SHIELD NUMBER 4:
# THE SHIELD
# OF RELATIONSHIPS

The shield of relationships is the outer shield. Not all companies can use it, but more can than do. It is the shield that lies in that area that defines the types of business relationships that your company desires. The shield of relationships is built upon the assumption that litigation may no longer be isolated to a particular transaction. Companies need to know that a lawsuit will probably undermine the entire relationship among them. Proper utilization of the shield of relationships involves a carrot-and-stick strategy. Let's start with the stick.

## THE STICK: NO NEW BUSINESS

Traditionally companies that did a lot of business with one another, particularly large multidivisional concerns, continued to do business even if they were in litigation over a discrete transaction. The companies would "agree to disagree" over the transaction in question, but it would be business as usual for their deals regarding other products or services. Often this approach was the most financially intelligent. Companies could isolate the problem and let the courts deal with it while continuing to profit from their relationship.

Recent changes in the nature of business litigation that we have discussed extensively in this book have rendered this containment policy obsolete in many, if not most, circumstances. For several reasons, isolation of litigation has become virtually impossible.

First, there is no longer any way to contain the costs of litigation. As you know, business lawsuits are far more expensive than they used to be. Even small-business disputes routinely cost tens of thousands of dollars to get through the court system. Moreover, the increasing use of the clever new legal tactics that we have discussed means that there may be a lot more money at stake in your case than there might have been twenty years ago for a similar case.

There is also no way to contain the impact that litigation will have on your company's operations. Lawsuits are much more disruptive to the company than they used to be. The other side will invariably make broad requests for documents covering the entire breadth of your company's activities. The other side will force you to make top executives available for hours or even days of depositions. Often the court will do little to stop these tactics.

A consistent theme of this book has been that business litigation has greater cross-transactional implications than it once had. If, for example, a company takes the position in a lawsuit that your subcontract created a fiduciary relationship or that your conversations with a customer constituted a tortious act, you now have to worry about similar allegations in all of your other contracts with that company. If the other side is saying that one contract does not mean what it says, then what is to stop it from saying the same thing about your other contracts?

> In today's environment, the best financial decision for a company faced with a lawsuit may be to end the relationship entirely. An opposing company should know that if it is going to use the legal process to stretch, twist, and distort one transaction, there will be no further deals. It is not the litigation per se that requires that the relationship end; rather, it is the effect of the lawsuit on the company and its transactional expectations as a whole that renders the relationship not worth pursuing.

If there is any potential future business, other companies will think long and hard about suing your company, but only if your company makes it clear that such a suit will end the prospect of a future business relationship. There have been companies that have threatened to file a *second suit* based on the defendant's refusal to do further business after the first suit. Assuming no antitrust problems, however, these suits have a very weak foundation in the law, which remains very strong across the country in holding that companies are free to deal or not deal with whomever they choose. Practically speaking, a company cannot expect to repair a relationship by filing a second lawsuit.

There are many methods that your company may use to effectuate the shield of relationships. Some are in the nature of contract clauses; others are more policy oriented. Let's go over a few of the more proven methods.

## CROSS-CONTRACT CLAUSES

If your company is a purchaser of goods, the law allows you to withhold payment under the contract for defective performance by the supplier. If the defective performance causes you greater damage, such as the extra cost of procuring the goods from someone else, you have to go to court to get that money. However, some companies now include "cross-contract offset" clauses in their agreements that allow a party that suffers a clear, provable loss under one agreement to deduct the amount of the loss from sums owed to the same party under another agreement. While I must warn that the validity of such clauses has not been fully tested in all states, they appear to be gaining acceptance and should be seriously considered by companies that want to deter lawsuits.

For example, I recently represented a company that was a major subcontractor to a prime on a highway construction project. On a different project to build a bridge, my client was the prime contractor and hired the other corporation as a subcontractor. This is a very common situation in the construction and manufacturing industries, among others. On the highway project, the other company acting as prime refused to pay my client $600,000 and sued my client, alleging all kinds of ridiculous tort theories.

On the bridge contract, in which my client was the prime, the other company performed its subcontracting duties quite well. However, my client had placed into the first contract a clause that said, "If the prime contractor fails to pay any of the sums due under this contract, [my client] may deduct the unpaid sum from any invoice due to the prime under any contract with [my client]." This is a cross-contract offset clause. My client then withheld the $600,000 due to the other company under the bridge subcontract, despite its virtually flawless performance.

The result was that the people at the other company who were performing the bridge subcontract so well became infuriated at not being paid for their admirable efforts, but they were not infuriated at us, they were infuriated at the people in their own company who had gotten them into such a mess! The other side quickly learned that litigation could not be contained to one transaction and would have a severely adverse effect upon the entire relationship between the parties.

Cross-contract offset clauses are becoming increasingly popular. Less common, and more controversial, are "cross-contract stop-work" clauses. The normal rule of law is that you may stop work on a contract if the other side commits a material breach of that contract. A cross-contract stop-work clause says you can stop work on all contracts that you have with a party if that party materially breaches one of them. Put simply, if you are not being paid on one project, you can stop working on all projects. Again, such a clause confirms that litigation is no longer about transactions, it is about relationships.

Cross-contract stop-work clauses are very severe and rarely used. Keep in mind that they are not permitted in some contracts, such as prime contracts and subcontracts in which the customer is the federal government. You should consider putting them in contracts and threaten to use them if necessary, but you should invoke them sparingly. Cross-contract stop-work clauses are particularly valuable for *providers* of goods and services because they can counterbalance cross-contract offset clauses that are most often used by *purchasers* of goods or services. Parties could even agree to include both clauses in their contracts as sort of mutual antilitigation devices. One side could stop payment on all contracts, and the other could stop work on all contracts. This constitutes high-stakes poker (almost "mutual assured destruction" in some cases), but it is undoubtedly a major deterrent to litigation.

## REQUESTS FOR ASSURANCES UNDER
## THE UNIFORM COMMERCIAL CODE

This is a nifty antilitigation device that I have used with success on a couple of occasions when the parties had extensive ongoing relationships involving agreements for the purchase of goods. The Uniform Commercial Code (UCC), which has been adopted in one form or another by all states, contains a provision that says a party is entitled to demand assurances that a business counterpart will perform its contracts any time that the conduct of the opposing party gives cause for "insecurity." For example, assume that one of your business counterparts starts taking positions in the performance of one contract that implicate the terms of other contracts. Maybe the other side is alleging that a contract modification clause or a termination clause is unenforceable. Your other contracts with the same company have the same clause in them. You should write a letter to the company citing the UCC, indicating that the company's positions on that contract have given you cause for insecurity on your other contracts. You should demand that the other side affirm the enforceability of the disputed terms in the other contracts, and require assurances that the other company will refrain from making allegations that these provisions are for any reason unenforceable.

The demand for assurances puts the other side in a catch-22. If the other company assures you that the clauses in question are enforceable on other contracts, it has undermined its position that the clauses are unenforceable with respect to the contract that is the subject of the dispute. To maintain its relationship with you, the company must undermine its allegation.

If, on the other hand, the other side refuses to give you the assurances that you requested, the UCC gives you all sorts of rights, including in appropriate cases the right to stop performance on all of the contracts for which you did not get the assurances. So the UCC can give you the equivalent of a "cross-contract stop-work" clause even if there is no such clause in your contracts.

It will be up to the business people to recognize situations in which another company's attitude about one contract has implications relative to the performance of other contracts. However, the process of demanding adequate assurances is a little tricky; there are a lot of "i's" to dot and "t's" to cross, so consult your company attorney before you

197

take any action. Often, it is a very effective way to proceed. Again, the demand for assurances to an adversary tells that company that the entire relationship is at stake. Anytime a company knows that its actions may end the relationship, it will give much more serious consideration to alternatives. Consequently, the UCC demand for assurances is a great deterrent to lawsuits.

## CORPORATE FAMILY RELATIONSHIPS

Corporations often have families. They have parent companies that own them; they may have sister companies that share a common holding company; and they may have subsidiaries, the corporate equivalent of children. These relationships are fair game as you erect the shield of relationships.

For example, recently an aerospace company made a series of outlandish public allegations against one of my clients. The company alleged that my client had "conspired" to "destroy" a potential program between that company and a foreign government. The company sought over $3 million from my client. We found the allegations outrageously false. We had no other business with that company that we could use as leverage to get it to cease making these allegations. Going to court appeared to be the only way to resolve the matter. However, my client's CEO sent out an e-mail asking all employees if they knew of any work being considered for this company. The responses revealed that a different division of my corporate client was negotiating a huge manufacturing licensing deal with the European parent company of our adversary. The European parent sought a license to manufacture a product of ours for sale to the same foreign government that the subsidiary accused us of manipulating! The deal was worth $70 million to the parent company.

A senior executive at my client's headquarters wrote the CEO of our adversary's parent company. The letter summarized the situation with the subsidiary and suggested that the parent company obviously did not want to do business with my client, a company that was, according to its own subsidiary, "conspiring" to "destroy" its programs with that foreign government. The letter concluded with the proposal to end the $70 million licensing agreement.

## SHIELD NUMBER 4: THE SHIELD OF RELATIONSHIPS

Within hours, we received a fax stating that the CEO of the parent company would have a little talk with the CEO of the subsidiary, and that the parent was certain that the parties could come to an understanding that would allow the licensing deal to go forward. The matter was settled quite favorably for my client soon thereafter. I wish I could have heard the conversation between the CEO of the parent when he called the CEO of the subsidiary to tell him that his ranting and raving over $3 million was about to cost the parent company a $70 million deal.

The point here is that the relationship at stake in a business dispute may be more than just the one between the two companies; it may involve affiliates. Your company, with legal guidance, needs to investigate this possibility thoroughly.


## THE CARROT:
## BUSINESS WITHOUT LAWSUITS

All of the tactics described above involve leveraging relationships to let a party know that it will suffer dearly if it sues you. But as you erect shield after shield, you need to consider the value of enticement. The possibility of a better relationship, one without lawsuits or even a litigious mind-set, is often what really ends up keeping ethical companies out of court for the long term. And perhaps that is the best way to end this book—with a little enticement.

Picture this scenario. Your company has a good program on how to avoid lawsuits, so your people no longer make many of the Eight Big Mistakes. They write better; they estimate better; they stick to their areas of expertise; they do more thorough research. If problems arise, they do not ignore them. They keep their emotions out of their meetings and letters; they do not make side deals. They are careful in the way in which they wield power.

Your people have also put up the shields very effectively. They take advantage of the attorney-client privilege to protect sensitive legal assessments, so the files are clean. Your employees only sign agreements that define intercorporate relationships carefully and that include all those clauses that make potential adversaries think twice before racing to the courthouse.

Then a big dispute arises between your company and a company with which it has done business for years. The other side threatens to sue. Your company personnel are confident that you can avoid a lawsuit because you have litigation-smart employees who do not generate bad evidence, and your contracts make litigation very risky for the other side.

So you follow the plan. You enter into a tolling agreement with the other company and invite the senior executives in for a presentation. Your presentation is flawless. The other side has very little to say because your people have not given it much ammunition. You finish your presentation, after which your senior executive tells the other side's senior executive that a lawsuit will end the extensive relationship between the parties, invoking the shield of relationships.

Well, that company has taken one heck of a licking. It might capitulate right there; or, to salvage some pride, it might wait a few weeks and slowly come around. It is clear, however, that you are going to win this case without ever setting foot in a courthouse.

Even when this occurs, and you "win," however, the ultimate result may not be the best for either side. I always recommend that the party that is playing its cards so deftly finish the process by using the shield of relationships in a positive way to look forward to a future relationship without litigation. At some point in the dispute, your company needs to do extensive research on the full capabilities of the other side and identify some possible future relationships. Then, whether it be at the senior executive presentation or some other negotiating session, you can finish with a discussion of what the relationship *could be* if the other side would come to its senses and settle the matter reasonably without a lawsuit.

If you have taken offsets or have told the other side that it is out of the running for future work, you should also consider informing the other side about upcoming projects that might be mutually profitable if the company can put the dispute behind it. How far you want to go in discussing future commitments depends on the circumstances, and whatever you agree upon must be clearly documented in a settlement agreement so that there can be no misunderstandings later. You can commit to appoint a person in each company to work on identifying or developing future business possibilities, or you can identify such work and actually spell it out in the settlement agreement.

Often giving a party additional business opportunities is the key factor to closing a settlement because that party can offset any write-off it has to take on the transaction in dispute with profits from the new work. If you do offer such opportunities, you may require that the individuals who caused the problems with the prior project not work on the new one. You may stipulate that the other side give you adequate assurances that both sides will give the same meaning and effect to key contract clauses that had been in dispute. You can include any caveats you need to be comfortable with a continued relationship.

If you really seek to avoid lawsuits over the long term, you will endeavor to resolve all disputes on a positive note. Even if you have positioned yourself so well that you can emerge the "victor" without ever going to court, you have not really won in the long run if you have lost even one potential supplier, customer, or trading counterpart.

So get to work and make your company suitproof. Educate rigorously, negotiate intelligently, protect the company diligently, and respond to threats strongly. And look for a resolution that takes everyone one step closer to a world of business without lawsuits.

# NOTES AND WORKS
# CONSULTED

## PART ONE

The statistics regarding the caseload in the federal courts come from *Federal Court Management Statistics* (1996) published by the Administrative Office of the United States Courts, Statistics Division, Thurgood Marshall Federal Judiciary Building, Washington, D.C. 20544. *See also Statistical Tables for the Federal Judiciary,* published by the same office.

The statistics regarding the legal costs incurred by companies with annual revenues of $1 to $2.5 billion and law firms used were compiled by and reprinted with the permission of Altman Weil Pensa, Inc., Two Campus Boulevard, Suite 200, Newtown Square, PA 19073, and published in its *Law Department Functions and Expenditures Report 1997 Survey* (draft).

The statistics about legal costs, pending litigation, and law firm usage by companies with annual revenues of $10 to $20 billion were compiled by and reprinted with the permission of Price Waterhouse LLP, Law Department Consulting Group, 1177 Avenue of the Americas, New York, NY 10036, and published in the *Price Waterhouse Law Department Spending Survey* (1996).

The statement that legal costs can amount to 5 to 10 percent of earnings for some companies is based on my comparison of the Price Waterhouse statistics on legal costs as a percentage of revenue with the earnings statements of participating companies, and on personal experience.

## PARTS TWO AND THREE

The discussion of the *Pinto* case as an example of the problems associated with estimating the value of life represents the "conventional wisdom" on the meaning and significance of that case, and is consistent with the writings of many commentators, including the California appellate court that affirmed the jury's punitive damages award. *See Grimshaw* v. *Ford Motor Co.,* 119 Cal. App. 3d

757, 810 (1981). However, one commentator has made a good case that, while the press and public were outraged by Ford's estimation of the value of life, the jury in that case did not make the decision on that basis because much of the evidence relative to Ford's policies was excluded by the trial judge from consideration. *See* "The Myth of the Ford Pinto Case" by Gary T. Schwartz, *Rutgers Law Review,* Summer 1991.

The statement that over 30 percent of résumés contain inaccurate information may well be conservative. The *Capital Times* used this figure in an article entitled "Background Checks Help Safeguard Companies," p. 1C, October 9, 1996. *See also* "On the Job: It's No Lie—Resume Padding Can Mean Lawsuits, Firings," *The Nashville Banner,* p. D1, August 21, 1996, citing research by the Society of Human Resource Management. The *Kansas City Star* stated that on average 30 percent of all information on résumés is falsified. *See* "Know the Risks of Resume Hype," p. D1, March 16, 1997, citing a study by Goodrich & Sherwood Assoc., Inc. Other published reports suggest that résumé fraud and misrepresentation are even more prevalent. *See* "Candid Candidates: What's Behind the Resume?" *Security Management,* Vol. 39, No. 5, p. 66 (1995) citing a *New Jersey Law Journal* study for the proposition that "75% of résumés contain some type of misrepresentation or erroneous data."

The statement that the government declines to intervene in over 75 percent of the False Claims Act whistle-blower suits is based upon data contained in "Whistleblower Bounty Lawsuits as Monitoring Devices in Government Contracting," by William E. Kovacic, *Loyola of Los Angeles Law Review,* Vol. 29, Issue No. 4, June 1996.

The Kansas judge who called UCC 2–207 a "murky bit of prose" did so in the case of *Southwest Engineering Co.* v. *Martin Tractor Co.,* 473, P.2d 18, 25 (1970).

Other works that I consulted in writing this book include (1) numerous federal and state court judicial opinions and pleadings; (2) several well-known treatises and legal reporters on the subject of product liability, antitrust, and contracts—most valuable was the *Restatement (2ⁿᵈ) of Contracts;* (3) *Black's Law Dictionary;* (4) research memoranda written by members of my firm on the subject of attorney-client privilege; and (5) stories from *The Wall Street Journal* and other leading newspapers.

# GLOSSARY

**Alternative dispute resolution (ADR).** A phrase that encompasses a variety of means to resolve legal disputes outside the judicial system. Arbitration and mediation are the two most common types of ADR.

**Antitrust laws.** Laws designed to protect companies and consumers from the effects of anticompetitive activity such as price-fixing, predatory pricing, and product tying, and conspiracies to monopolize.

**Arbitrary factor.** The chance that you will win or lose a case regardless of the merits of your position due to tactics of counsel, the overloaded judiciary, nebulous legal causes of action, and the unpredictability of juries.

**Arbitration.** A process to resolve disputes that involves the presentation of the case for decision to a neutral person who does not have judicial authority over the matter. In binding arbitration, the decision of the neutral party can be enforced in court. In baseball arbitration, the arbitrator has to make an all-or-nothing decision in favor of one party.

**Attorney-client privilege.** The client's ability to refuse to disclose or permit disclosure of confidential communications to his or her attorney made for the purpose of securing legal advice.

**Battle of the forms.** A term used by lawyers and judges to describe a common business practice whereby parties intending to form a contract send differing and sometimes conflicting form agreements to each other.

**Burden of proof.** The requirement that a party establish a stated degree of belief in the mind of the judge or jury that a particular fact is true. In civil cases, the burden of proof is normally a preponderance of the evidence, commonly stated to be "most" of the evidence. In criminal cases, the burden of proof is evidence beyond a reasonable doubt, which has been described as an "overwhelming" level of evidence.

# GLOSSARY

**Buy in.** The decision by a company to enter into a transaction with the knowledge that it will probably lose money, but with the hope that it will gain a contractual or marketing advantage that will allow it to profit in future related transactions.

**Capability speculation.** A statement that involves an assessment of the ability of a person or company to perform a job, made by a person who is not the most qualified to make the statement.

**Compensatory damages.** Damages that remedy the injury sustained by a party but do not provide additional sums to punish the offending party.

**Compliance program.** A set of policies and procedures, usually developed by counsel after the study of the laws, regulations, and legal issues applicable to a client, which assists employees in maintaining high legal and ethical standards of conduct.

**Contract of adhesion.** A take-it-or-leave-it form contract provided by a company to a consumer.

**Corporation.** A legal entity defined by state law that generally has rights and duties similar to those of a person—the right to contract, hold real estate, etc. The corporate structure, if properly used, also limits the legal liability of individual shareholders and employees.

**Critical path.** The chain of events that drives progress toward the ultimate transactional objective.

**Cross-contract clause.** A term contained in one contract that expressly allows a party to take action under another contract between the same parties when a specified event occurs. A cross-contract offset clause permits a nonbreaching party to deduct sums owed by it under one contract to compensate for sums owed by the breaching party under another contract.

**Cybertransaction.** A "paperless" transaction that is negotiated, transmitted, consummated, and stored exclusively through the use of computers.

**Deposition.** Pretrial testimony taken under oath as part of the discovery process.

**Discovery.** The process of using legal devices such as interrogatories, depositions, and requests for production of documents to obtain information about the case prior to trial.

**Duty.** In law, the legal obligation that comes with a right.

# GLOSSARY

**Early neutral evaluation (ENE).** The use of a neutral third party other than the assigned judge to evaluate the merits of a case after a presentation by each side.

**Environmental law.** The body of statutes, regulations, and interpretive judicial opinions related to the use and disposal of toxic substances and the protection of the environment.

**Fiduciary relationship.** A relationship between two persons or entities concerning a business or an estate such that one or both parties put trust or confidence in the other, and such that a party in whom such trust is placed must exercise a high degree of fairness and good faith in all dealings with the other party.

**File-retention audit.** A formally scheduled review of files to determine whether they should or must be kept or discarded.

**Forum-selection clause.** A contract term that requires legal actions to be filed in a stated geographical area and/or in a particular type of court, e.g., state court, federal court, or international court.

**Four corners doctrine.** An evidentiary rule and phrase commonly used by lawyers meaning that contracts should be interpreted by looking at all of their terms together and not in isolation, but that extracontractual statements and understandings should not be used to interpret otherwise clear contract language.

**Fraud.** An intentional misrepresentation made to induce another person or entity to give up something of value.

**Hostile environment.** A concept in employment discrimination law that can be generally defined as workplace atmosphere that is degrading to women or minorities.

**Implied contract.** A contract that arises by reason of conduct rather than oral or written commitments.

**In-house counsel.** A lawyer who is employed to work exclusively for a certain corporation rather than for multiple clients on a case-by-case basis.

**Insider trading.** Stock transactions by people who have information not available to the public made on the basis of such information.

**Integration rule.** The presumption that a contract is the entire agreement between the parties regarding its subject matter.

# GLOSSARY

**Invitee.** A person who enters a company's premises at the request of the owner or the owner's agent in connection with the transaction of the owner's business.

**Joint defense privilege.** An extension of the attorney-client privilege to communications between multiple parties and their counsel when they have common interests to defend themselves against a civil or criminal investigation or action.

**Learning curve.** The rate of increased efficiency achieved by making a product or performing a service more than one time.

**Liability speculation.** Conjecture by people other than lawyers as to the party that is legally responsible for damages incurred by another party.

**Liquidated damages.** A specific sum of money that contracting parties agree on as the recovery for a breach, should such a breach occur in the future. It is enforceable only if it attempts to approximate the actual damages that will be incurred.

**Litigation.** The process of filing a lawsuit, developing information about the other side's case, preparing the case for trial before a judge or jury, and, if necessary, appealing the verdict or judgment to a higher court.

**Management challenge.** An effort by management to encourage employees to find ways to cut the cost of performance below that which was estimated for the job.

**Market-effect resolution.** A means of identifying and resolving workplace problems by looking at their effect on corporate productivity rather than their ethical or moral implications.

**Mediation.** The use by disputing parties of a neutral third party to facilitate a resolution.

**Negligence.** The failure to use reasonable care in one's actions.

**Obstruction of justice.** The intentional and improper interference with the progress of a government investigation.

**Outside counsel.** A lawyer who is not an employee of an organization who is retained by the organization to provide legal services.

**Parole evidence rule.** A legal doctrine that precludes the use of extracontractual oral or written statements to alter the express terms of a contract.

# GLOSSARY

**Partnership.** In its purely legal sense, a business relationship between two or more individuals who agree to work together toward a common goal without forming a corporation but by undertaking fiduciary duties toward one another. Often used informally to describe cooperation between companies without a fiduciary relationship.

***Prima facie* tort.** A lawful act done without justification for the purpose of inflicting harm on another.

**Prime contractor.** An individual or entity that has a contract with a customer to provide goods and services. A *subcontractor* is under contract to provide goods and services to the prime contractor for its use in the performance of the prime contract.

**Probability speculation.** A prediction of the likelihood of an occurrence made by a person who is not the best qualified to make such a judgment.

**Proprietary information.** Information such as a secret formula, technology, or financial data that, if released publicly, would damage the competitive interests of a party that owns or lawfully holds the information.

**Punitive damages.** A sum awarded against a party to punish it for intentional wrongdoing.

**Risk assessment.** In the context of this book, the use of counsel to investigate and advise a company of the possible liability or recovery associated with an actual or potential business dispute, and to recommend means by which to reduce the potential liability or increase the potential recovery.

**Rule.** An inflexible requirement (in contrast to "standard").

**Self-evaluative privilege.** A legal privilege that sometimes permits an entity to refrain from disclosing to third parties certain limited types of documents and communications that relate to internal corporate evaluation.

**Senior official presentation.** A form of dispute resolution in which each side presents its case to senior corporate officials, both of whom have otherwise been uninvolved in the dispute. The officials then meet in private to attempt to reach a settlement.

**Settlement privilege.** A rule which varies in different states and courts but that generally prevents an offer of compromise (such as a proposed cash settlement) from being admissible in court to prove the liability of the offeror.

**Shareholders' derivative suit.** An action brought by shareholders against the company (and usually its directors and officers) alleging misuse of information to the detriment of the company or severe mismanagement of the company in violation of fiduciary duties.

**Standard.** A flexible measure of conduct, not a rule.

**Statute of frauds.** A law that describes the circumstances under which unwritten agreements will be legally enforceable.

**Statute of limitations.** The period of time during which a particular type of suit must be filed.

**Strict liability.** Legal responsibility imposed without proof of fault.

**Subpoena.** The use of the legal process to compel testimony. Also the document served upon a party whose testimony is being compelled.

**Summary judgment.** Judgment in favor of a party before trial because the court determines that there is no material issue of fact for a jury or the court to decide at trial.

**TBD.** Literally, "to be determined." In the context of contract formation, a term or value in the contract that is omitted at the time the contract is signed or otherwise agreed upon, and that the parties agree will be added later.

**Team.** A legal commitment between two entities to work together, usually as equals, pursuant to the terms of a teaming agreement. Often used informally to indicate two companies that are cooperating with each other.

**Termination clause.** A contract term that allows one or both parties to end the contract prior to the completion of performance. A termination for convenience clause allows termination even when the terminated party has performed the contract properly. A termination for default clause or termination for cause clause allows termination only upon the occurrence of specified acts of misfeasance or nonperformance.

**Tolling agreement.** An agreement to stop temporarily the statute of limitations from running on a claim. Usually made while settlement discussions are going on in order to allow parties to preserve their rights.

**Tort.** An action causing injury resulting from the breach of a general legal duty that is independent of the terms or duties imposed by a legal agreement. Intentional torts are deliberate wrongful acts such as assault and fraud.

# GLOSSARY

**Unfair competition.** A nebulous intentional tort involving dishonest trade practices designed to hurt a competitor, most frequently the imitation of another's product through deceptive means.

**Uniform Commercial Code (UCC).** A legal code drafted by the National Conference of Commissioners on Uniform State Laws and the American Law Institute governing commercial transactions. The UCC has been adopted in some form by all fifty states.

**Value definition.** As used in this book, a contract term that allows the other side the option to buy a proprietary right and thereby values that right.

**Voluntary disclosure.** As used in this book, the decision by a corporation to disclose a known wrong to government authorities with the hope or expectation of more lenient treatment.

**Waiver.** The express or implied relinquishment of a known right.

**Work product privilege.** The client's limited privilege not to disclose to third parties materials prepared in anticipation of litigation. Can be invalidated by a court when the other side shows undue hardship caused by not having the materials.

# INDEX

# INDEX